Live Oak Splendor

Live Oak Splendor

GARDENS ALONG THE MISSISSIPPI,
FROM NATCHEZ TO NEW ORLEANS

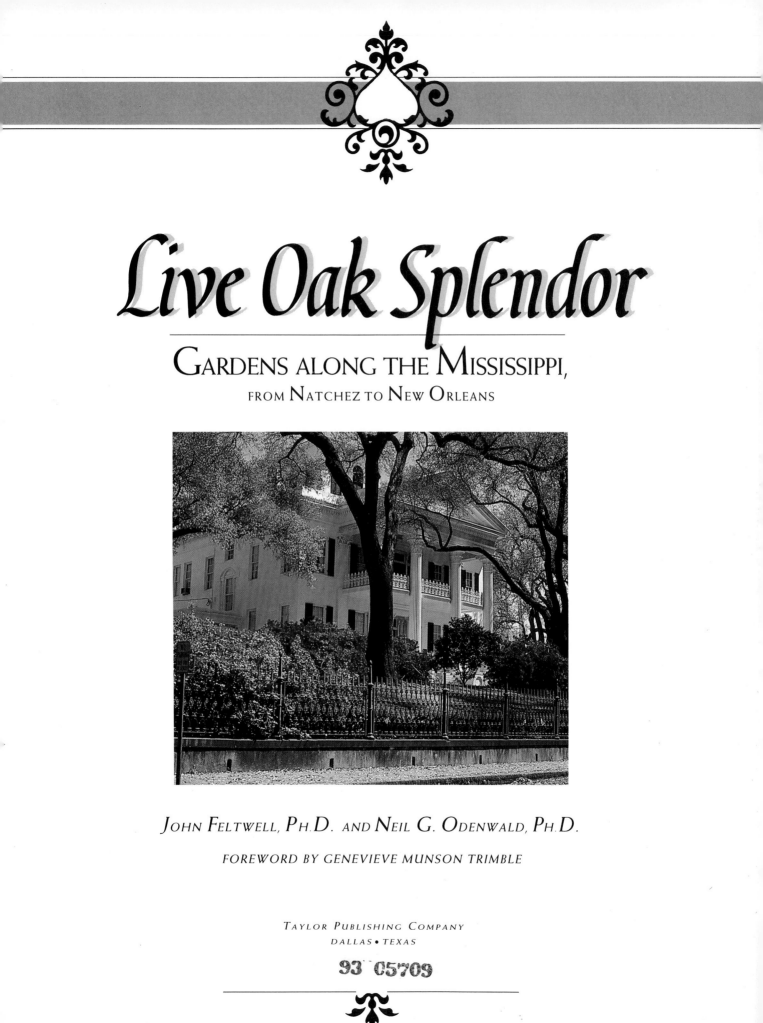

JOHN FELTWELL, PH.D. AND NEIL G. ODENWALD, PH.D.

FOREWORD BY GENEVIEVE MUNSON TRIMBLE

TAYLOR PUBLISHING COMPANY
DALLAS • TEXAS

PHOTOGRAPHY

MOST OF THE COLOR ILLUSTRATIONS IN THIS BOOK WERE TAKEN BY
JOHN FELTWELL ON A BRONICA AE II MEDIUM FORMAT CAMERA WITH A 50
MM LENS. THEY WERE ALL TAKEN USING FUJICHROME 100 ASA RDP FILM, MOST
AT F.22, ALL FROM A TRIPOD. THREE TRIPS WERE NECESSARY TO COVER
THE SEASONS AND COLORS, AND THESE OCCURRED IN NOVEMBER 1990, MARCH
1991, AND JULY 1991. THE PICTURES USED WERE SELECTED FROM ABOUT
EIGHT THOUSAND. AERIAL PICTURES WERE TAKEN FROM A CESSNA 152.

PUBLISHED BY TAYLOR PUBLISHING COMPANY
1550 WEST MOCKINGBIRD LANE
DALLAS, TEXAS 75235

DESIGNED BY LURELLE CHEVERIE

LIBRARY OF CONGRESS CATALOGING-IN-PUBLICATION DATA

ODENWALD, NEIL G.
    LIVE OAK SPLENDOR : GARDENS ALONG THE MISSISSIPPI FROM NATCHEZ TO
NEW ORLEANS./ NEIL G. ODENWALD, JOHN FELTWELL.
    P.   C.M.
    INCLUDES INDEX.
    ISBN 0-87833-807-1
    1. GARDENS—LOUISIANA—PICTORIAL WORKS. 2. GARDENS—MISSISSIPPI
RIVER REGION—PICTORIAL WORKS. 3. GARDENS—MISSISSIPPI—PICTORIAL
WORKS. I. FELTWELL, JOHN. II. TITLE.
SB466.U65L686 1992
712'.09763—DC20   92-13054
                                                        CIP
PRINTED IN THE UNITED STATES OF AMERICA
10 9 8 7 6 5 4 3 2 1

Sponsors

JEFFERSON PARISH ADOPT-A-PARKWAY

*T*he Jefferson Parish Adopt-A-Parkway program is an organization of volunteers who work with the Parish Parkway Department in beautifying and maintaining public green spaces.

SOUTHERN GARDEN SYMPOSIUM
ST. FRANCISVILLE, LOUISIANA

*T*he Southern Garden Symposium seeks to preserve and commemorate the gardening traditions of the Deep South through lectures, workshops, and tours of historic gardens. Its aim is to nurture knowledge of the past while interpreting this lore to an interested public.

Contents

Foreword

I n 1835, Joseph Holt Ingraham, a sojourner from Maine, traveling by steamboat up the Mississippi from New Orleans to Natchez, made this rueful observation:

> In America where vegetation is on a scale of magnificence commensurate with her continental extent, it is remarkable that a taste for horticulture should be so little cultivated. The grandeur of the forests in the South, and the luxuriance of the shrubs and plants, have no parallel. But Southerners tread the avenues, breathe the air, and recline under the trees and arbours of their paradise, thankfully accepting and enjoying their luxurious boon, but seldom insinuating, through the cultivation of flowers, that nature has left her work imperfect. As a general rule, Southerners, with the exception of the cultivation of a few plants in the front yard, pay little regard to horticulture. [Yet] though Southerners do not often pursue horticulture as a science, they are passionately fond of flowers. The South is emphatically the land of flowers; nature seems to have turned this region from her hand as the *chef d'oeuvre* of her skill.
>
> The race here now is for wealth, but in good time the passion will change. And horticulture will then shed its genial influence over the valley of the South, with the existence of that fine taste, in the germ at least, which refinement, opulence, and leisure will in time unfold and ripen to maturity.

Little could this Yankee traveler have known that, even as he wound up the river, a great plantation garden era was already emerging and that the very plantations he passed would all too soon, as if in answer, be flowering visions of his prophecy.

*H*e was too early, for instance, to view the work of Valcour Aime, who, but seven years later on his plantation at the turn of the river below Vacherie, would break ground for his French *Jardin Anglais*, so dazzling an accomplishment that it would be nicknamed by awed visitors *Le Petit Versailles* and establish him in history as the "Louis XIV of Louisiana."

Nor could Ingraham have known the likes of such budding gardeners as Martha Turnbull, who in 1835, the very year Ingraham passed her plantation a stone's throw from the river at St. Francisville, was already plotting out her fabulous gardens at Rosedown.

The passionate pursuit of wealth, which Ingraham observed, would indeed, once realized, soon open up to these provincial planters limitless horizons of refinement, opulence, and leisure. Traveling abroad extensively, they would bring back dreams of the splendid pleasure gardens they had visited in England, France, and Italy, and which they eagerly translated amidst their live oaks and lush greenery into a style so uniquely theirs that by their heyday, in the 1850s, these gardens would speak in a vernacular all their own and for all time. Not even subsequent wars, economic disasters, or heartbreaking years of neglect would obliterate the mystique of the fabled antebellum plantation gardens of the lower Mississippi River.

Now, more than 150 years later, John Feltwell and Neil Odenwald, seasoned guides of the landscape, retrace Ingraham's route to take us on a magical river voyage from New Orleans to Natchez, to see what has transpired through the years, to record the imprint of the historical garden tradition upon this rich river region, and to report on the present-day state of the garden and the direction in which it is moving.

What do they find? What has changed? What remains the same? In the distance, one can still see some of the old enchantments, gardens of a past grandeur, symbols in themselves of the insistence of gardens on changing with time to reflect the passing eras. But equally exciting and coming into view is a new landscape toward which the authors point: a new age and rage for gardening, growing out of the old tradition, that now rejuvenates the lower Mississippi River region.

*T*here can be no doubt that, since the 1950s, we have been in the midst of an unbelievable reawakening of garden interest. What has brought about this invigorating movement? A number of likely influences: growing public awareness of our precious environment with its vanishing, oft manhandled greenspace, and a new desire to protect and nurture it; a newborn urge to get back to our roots and to learn of our horticultural heritage; and an emerging attitude that gardens, once the indulgence of the wealthy, can now easily be a rewarding possession of all.

Gone perhaps are most of the vast legendary gardens requiring a corps of gardeners for maintenance. But springing up out of the foundation of old garden practices and old plant culture is a remarkable array of new twentieth-century pleasure gardens—more manageable, more easily kept and enjoyed by the individual: the wildflower garden, the small backyard walled or fenced garden, the patio, the container garden, the special collections of gardeners who in the interest of practicality and space confine their interest to one species, be it camellias, daffodils, daylilies, irises, roses, or azaleas. There is a trend even among those who do not own an inch of ground to become themselves "friends of the garden" and to volunteer their hours and talents toward maintaining such important publicly visited gardens as Oakley, Oak Alley, Longue Vue Gardens, the New Orleans Botanical Garden, and many others like them.

Admissions to these gardens, records show, are on an increase. Garden and horticultural groups abound. Flower and plant markets and nurseries prosper. Garden symposia such as the Southern Garden Symposium held each October in St. Francisville play to standing room only and bring to the area an influx of notable gardeners, horticulturists, and ideas from afar.

With great charm and expertise, authors Feltwell and Odenwald chronicle this spectacular resurgence in gardening as they explore the past and present and beautifully illustrate how horticulture, true to Ingraham's prediction, now "sheds its genial influence over the valley of the South."

An hour spent with this book can make the reader at once more knowledgeable about and prouder of this region's heritage, more inspired by the beauty of this environment, and more zealous to protect it. It will surely entice even the most reluctant to wander out of doors to explore anew the charm, romance, and elegance of gardening along the lower Mississippi, rooted in the past, ever-evolving, and growing toward its place in the twenty-first century.

Look forward, dear reader, turn the page—the best is yet to come!

GENEVIEVE MUNSON TRIMBLE
AFTON VILLA,
ST. FRANCISVILLE
AUTUMN, 1992

Preface

ow could two men separated by the Atlantic Ocean and more, with widely different backgrounds and experiences, come together on a collaborative project like writing a book on gardening? By chance or providential appointment? It all began during a late afternoon conversation on the porch of The Cottage near St. Francisville following a Friday workshop session of the 1990 Southern Gardening Symposium. While enjoying a glass of lemonade provided by our hostess, Mary Brown, châtelaine at that wonderful early nineteenth-century house, right in the midst of the southern landscape, we began discussing our mutual interest in gardening and in particular a very special region of the South—the stretch of country along the Mississippi River from Natchez to New Orleans. Without a lot of fanfare, no contract, and just a handshake, what started out as an uncertain venture soon blossomed into a wonderful friendship and has been a most remarkable experience for us during the intervening eighteen months of work on *Live Oak Splendor*.

While titles have been keenly debated and changed frequently, there has been a common theme and focus during all our work: sharing with the people of the area, and especially our friends and welcomed visitors, the joys and enthusiasm for a region that has enjoyed a rich and dynamic heritage for more than two hundred years. Love of gardening is still very much alive and thriving here. With each generation, a new layer is added. We reflect on the past and explore contemporary trends in the hope that readers will reach a better understanding of gardens of the past and present, and will join the host of people who love to garden.

Gardening for us is not new. Although coming to this subject from widely different life experiences, we converge at a point in our lives when we recognize that we have been most fortunate to have had unique opportunities to visit and revisit gardens of the lower Mississippi region, many of which are not open to the public, but where owners have graciously opened their "garden gates" to us, sometimes for quick glimpses and at other times for rather extended photographing sessions. Every visit has been a learning experience.

*F*or me (John), my journey to horticulture began from the world of entomology. After graduating at the University of London in entomology in 1970 and then with a Ph.D. in botany in 1973, I spent a few years teaching botany at a United Kingdom public (meaning private) school. In 1980, I became a freelance lecturer for various U.K. universities, photographer, leader of wildlife tours, and above all a freelance author. I have broadened my experience on ecological issues which impinge upon gardening with fact-finding trips to the virgin rainforests of southeast Asia and to the American deserts. In the last ten years I have published more than twenty books for children and adults on general natural history, ecology, conservation, and gardening. While still retaining an interest in insects, especially butterflies, I have moved in recent years further into the field of garden design; indeed I am now the principal lecturer for the University of Kent's diploma in garden history, management, and design.

The germ of this book was set on a ten-thousand-mile grand tour of the United States during 1989 (July, September, November) when I visited more than two hundred mostly private gardens in twenty-two states from Maine to Florida and all the southern states from east to west. This unique foray to the best of America's gardens opened my eyes to one part of the country distinctly different from the rest: the Mississippi River corridor. It was as if this area had been bypassed by the gardening connoisseurs—it didn't have the instant nouveau gardens of the West, or the woodland gardens of much of the eastern seaboard, and it didn't have the dry heat of Florida with its tropicals and subtropicals. It had a unique climate, topography, and lifestyle, and, for me, as a francophile, it had an appealing connection with France. The gardens were spectacularly formal and strongly European. There was an air of grandeur and pomp in the magnificent gardens that would match any garden in the northeast. These gardens had presence, they had distinctive character, with their great trees festooned with Spanish moss, and they were very special.

*T*o an outsider such as myself, the striking things about the region include the apparent cocooned time-warp in which the gardens exist, the extremely rich heritage of garden history, the exuberance and variety of plant growth, the taming of the mighty river in juxtaposition to the gardens, and the pleasant southern ambience. Nowhere else in the United States could you find any garden like this. A book had to be conceived to let everyone else know about the riches of the South. Mary Helen Ray of Savannah originally directed me to this region, but the happy event which made all this possible was my chance meeting with Mr. and Mrs. Morrell Trimble on my grand tour and their introducing me to Neil Odenwald. The concept of the book gelled as soon as Neil and I started talking.

*F*or me (Neil), the pilgrimage began back in the Mississippi Delta, only a few miles from the Mississippi River, but somewhat upstream from our area of special focus in this book. At Heathman, in the heart of cotton country, where thousands of acres of cotton and other row crops grow, it was Mrs. A. G. Nash who unknowingly challenged me by example to grow my first garden plants. I thought she had the most beautiful nasturtiums in all the world, although that "world" was indeed quite small for me at the time. The seed was planted, and for the next fifty years, plants, gardening, and design have been a passion and have brought me some of life's richest rewards. First it was gardening at home, then off to Mississippi State College where I enjoyed both undergraduate and Ph.D. work in a stimulating horticulture program under the direction of the late Professor Coy Box, with later work in landscape design under Professor Edward C. Martin, Jr.

At Louisiana State University, an entirely new phase in my appreciation of the natural world began. Doctor Robert S. "Doc" Reich introduced a fascinating world of challenge and opportunities—that of design and using plants in artistic expression to provide fuller meaning to people using outdoor spaces, as well as a more sympathetic stewardship of nature's vast resources.

More than all of the classroom and other academic pursuits combined, it was travel that sharpened my sensitivity and awareness, and made me even more curious about nature and our

relationship to the natural environment. By visiting widely diverse landscapes of the world with equally varied and interesting cultures and heritages, I have come to appreciate in a new and refreshing way our own unique gardening heritage.

*T*wenty years with students in the classroom and associations with the LSU faculty have added other special rewards. In recent years I have been particularly fortunate to be the landscape architectural consultant for some of the region's finest public and private gardens, many of which are included in this book. Working on sites with individual clients, gardening committees, and especially the resident gardeners has given me the finest learning experiences one could hope to have. Learning, sharing, and experimenting embody the true spirit of gardening. We have had lots of successes, and although sometimes we fail, we always come back to the source of one of life's most enjoyable experiences—gardening.

Acknowledgments

The authors gratefully acknowledge the contributions of a host of individuals and groups who have supported us. From Natchez to New Orleans and all points in between, we have received cordial receptions from members of the academic community, gardeners, librarians, friends, and family—all freely sharing technical and practical information on countless subjects, as well as being sources of enormous inspiration. To all those who will not find their names in print and possibly even unknowingly shared their love and enthusiasm for gardening through the years, you too are included.

Gardeners by nature are sharing people, and we particularly acknowledge the positive responses which property owners in the region made to our requests to visit and photograph their gardens. Unfortunately, we were able to include in the book photographs for only a small portion of the gardens visited. However, others are stored in special memories—memories we hope can be shared in another book. While we have attempted to credit the owners of all gardens included, be reassured that you, in particular, have made the book possible because of your generosity.

Genevieve Munson Trimble has been a constant source of support and inspiration during all phases of book preparation. We appreciate her willingness to join our team and write the foreword. Few people possess such enthusiasm for gardening. For Gen Trimble, theory becomes real life and practice in her New Orleans garden and beloved Afton Villa, a garden renewal project shared with her husband and gardening companion, Morrell (Bud) Trimble, "Master Pruner." Gen Trimble is the author of the *Gardener's Guide* and *Longue Vue*.

Our two book sponsors, the Adopt-A-Parkway program of Jefferson Parish Beautification Council and the Southern Garden Symposium, provided the funds to make possible John

Feltwell's visits to the United States. This financial assistance allowed the authors to spend valuable time together on issues directly related to the production of the manuscript. Without such support, the book may never have been possible.

JoAnn Christopher, Beulah Oswald, and landscape architect Rene Fransen spent numerous hours directing us from one garden to another during a memorable spring garden tour in New Orleans and Metairie, in addition to providing important contacts. Christopher Friedrichs, New Orleans landscape architect and authority on *Vieux Carré* courtyards and designer for many New Orleans gardens, was most helpful with work in the French Quarter. James Fondren, New Orleans landscape architect, shared valuable information on early plantation life, particularly at Houmas House. Special thanks are due Mrs. Glenda Haltom of Natchez who introduced John to many of the gardening joys in the area of Natchez and other points south in 1989 and 1990.

Landscape Architecture Professor Jack Haynes and Ferrell Jones, Research Assistant in the College of Design CADIS (computer) lab at Louisiana State University, provided tremendous assistance with technical problems relating to translating computer compatibility and communications between the authors in England and the United States.

David Floyd loaned us old and highly prized horticulture and medical books from his personal library. In addition, he provided insight on several early gardening topics. Martha White was most helpful with information on recipes and sources of photographs. Selma Sheriff "tidied" several Baton Rouge gardens for photographic sessions, shared a wealth of information on garden plants, and made valuable contacts for garden visits. *T*he staff at many of the gardens were most cordial and helpful during our on-site visits. Particular thanks go to Ivy and James Jones of Afton Villa, Carolyn Pittman and Cordell Veal at Rosedown, and John Harris at Longue Vue Gardens.

Colleagues on the faculty of the LSU School of Landscape Architecture have always been most helpful, and willingly supplied advice and wise counsel upon request. The authors acknowledge the expert assistance that Greg Grant provided in the identification of heirloom plants in gardens throughout the region.

The authors would also like to extend special thanks to

Wanda Barber and Martha White in Louisiana and Lee Ann Feltwell in Philadelphia for critically reading the manuscript and for offering their helpful comments.

And to our families, whose love, support, and patience helped to make all of this possible.

A special cadre of faithful friends and supporters:

Sadik Artunc	*Brandon Parlange*
Douglas Baker	*Sue Peters*
Dr. Elizabeth Boggess	*Faye Phillips*
Steele Burden	*Dr. Thomas E. Pope*
Cynthia Cash	*Mary Helen Ray*
Beverly Coates	*Dr. Robert S. Reich*
Max Conrad	*Bruce Sharky*
Dr. Daniel W. Earle	*Larry Smart*
Jon Emerson	*Debra Smith*
Margaret Groves	*Lou Riddle*
Susan and Jim Haltom	*Vi Stone*
Pam Hayne	*Flo Treadway*
Hilary S. Irvin	*Suzanne Turner*
Edward C. Martin, Jr.	*Dr. William C. Welch*
Sandra T. Mooney	*"Shingo" Woodward*
Ava Lisa Moore	*Wayne Womack*
Madeline Nevill	

*W*e would like to thank the Hill Memorial Library for photos of Oak Alley, Houmas House, and plans of Valcour Aime and Magnolia Vale, the LSU library for use of photographic material from the Theodore Landry Collection, *Fine Gardening* for the photograph of the Emerson/Womack garden, and Random House for permission to quote from Russell Page's *The Education of a Gardener.*

The Setting

GARDENS ALONG THE MISSISSIPPI RIVER CORRIDOR

Plantations near this situation

are superb indeed. The buildings upon

them evince [sic] great wealth and

refinement in modes of living. The

enclosed fields are very spacious

and highly cultivated.

FORTESCUE CUMING • 1810

gardening renaissance is sweeping the Mississippi River corridor. This two-hundred-mile stretch of unique southern landscape, beginning at Natchez situated high on the bluffs and surrounded by picturesque rolling hills, extends along the river to the fertile Mississippi Delta and New Orleans to the south. The renaissance involves restored gardens, their marvels and wonders, interwoven with the working life of plantations, which peaked in splendor in the 1850s.

The history of the region has been a tumultous one, admittedly. Following an early phase of competition for it by Spanish and French colonists who dislodged the aboriginal inhabitants and established New Orleans as a key New World entrepôt port, the area passed into United States ownership with the Louisiana Purchase in 1803. It was an era of slavery, with all its agonies and miseries—and, of course, prosperity for slave owners. While not wishing to celebrate the nature of that prosperous society, one can today appreciate the heritage of beauty it left behind in landscape architecture; and that heritage is now available to all in many public places.

The Civil War took its toll on the great estates of the Mississippi corridor, and for almost a century the local economy was effectively in a holding pattern. Following World War II, the region experienced a tumultuous upsurge of activity in building construction with rapid industrial development and expansion. For a time it seemed that most of the wonderful nature and

SET BENEATH THE GARLANDED BRANCHES OF TWO-HUNDRED-YEAR-OLD LIVE OAKS, PARLANGE

PLANTATION HAS HARDLY CHANGED IN THE 174 YEARS SINCE IT WAS BUILT. (NEW ROADS)

VERY FEW GARDENS ALONG THE MISSISSIPPI ESCAPE THE INFLUENCE OF THE MIGHTY LIVE OAKS, NATIVE TO THE REGION. LIVE OAKS GIVE SHADE AS WELL AS BEAUTY IN THEIR DELIGHTFULLY WANDERING LIMBS—BOTH QUALITIES ENCAPSULATED IN THE ALLÉES SO OFTEN SEEN ON THE GRAND ESTATES.

agricultural landscapes and gardens would be overrun and totally engulfed by industrial proliferation—primarily petrochemical complexes. Yet they endure.

Gardens along the Mississippi have a special southern grace and elegance. The river flows steadily past as it always has, and the essential charm of many plantation house and garden settings has changed little. Some the modern world has barely touched: the same old Spanish moss seems to hang from the serene live oaks. Time has been very gentle and kind to the plantations, but the plant growth has been quite extraordinary.

A new generation and an awakening in house and garden

A SLAVE HOUSE RECONSTRUCTION (1925) BY STEELE BURDEN AT THE RURAL LIFE MUSEUM IN BATON ROUGE. RESTORATION AND CONSERVATION OF HISTORIC GARDEN BUILDINGS HAS TAKEN PLACE FOR YEARS AT THE MUSEUM UNDER THE CARE OF ITS FOUNDER, STEELE BURDEN. BURDEN STARTED DESIGNING THE FORMAL GARDEN ON THE 450-ACRE BURDEN RESEARCH PLANTATION SITE AROUND 1930. TODAY THE GARDEN IS A SMALL PART OF THE MUSEUM, WHICH CONSISTS OF THREE AREAS. THE BARN CONTAINS THOUSANDS OF ARTIFACTS DEALING WITH EVERYDAY RURAL LIFE THROUGH THE AGES. THE WORKING PLANTATION INCLUDES A COMPLEX OF BUILDINGS AUTHENTICALLY RECONSTRUCTED TO REFLECT ALL THE MAJOR ACTIVITIES OF LIFE ON A TYPICAL NINETEENTH-CENTURY PLANTATION. LOUISIANA FOLK ARCHITECTURE IS EXEMPLIFIED IN SEVEN BUILDINGS THAT REFLECT THE VARIOUS CULTURES OF LOUISIANA SETTLERS.

restoration has brought some of these Louisiana and Mississippi gems to life. The garden history locked up in these homes and gardens is stupendous.

There is a passion for gardening in this region. People here have a rich tradition of working the land and growing agricultural crops like cotton, corn, sugar cane, tobacco, and soy bean, and managing forests and wetlands. A natural love of plants is characteristic of the culture. Gardening interests vary, from modest container gardening—claimed by nearly every household—to various specialty collections like camellias, daylilies, and azaleas, to planting and managing the more sophisticated gardens associated with plantations and urban centers.

Few people in the rest of the country, or even the world, have the opportunity to garden in such rich soil under subtropical conditions. The Mississippi is the third-largest river in the world, and has deposited some of the finest alluvial soils that gardeners could ever desire. Through the centuries plants have further improved the growing conditions by depositing a relatively high level of humus and abundant nutrients.

Plants grow at a phenomenal rate in this part of the South, perhaps five times the rate of those in the more temperate and arid sections of the United States or even in western Europe and the Mediterranean. Thanks to these soils, the ample supply of water, and a long growing season with relatively mild winters (although there are periodic extremes in temperature), gardeners enjoy an abundant palette of flora with a flowering period for both native and introduced species running for virtually the entire year.

We explore three types of gardens in this book: the intimate and enchanting private gardens of New Orleans; the plantation gardens closely associated with the river and the economic heyday of this region; and some remarkable contemporary suburban gardens in the greater New Orleans metropolitan area, Baton Rouge, Natchez, and the smaller, more rural communities along the river corridor. These newer gardens reflect a broad spectrum of lifestyles and gardening interests. They, too, have emerged in recent years from a strong influence in gardening history, with roots deeply embedded in the European, Colonial, and classical styles. We have thus included both gardens reflecting period styles and gardens that provide a unique sense of place.

New Orleans is a green city full of botanical fascination, punctuated with cloistered courtyards and small sites where gardening is practiced to a fine art. Cityscapes include intricately worked gardens and little vignettes that can be savored by passersby. It has been said that New Orleans, a city eternally in bloom,

THOUSANDS OF AZALEAS HAVE BEEN USED IN THE RECREATION OF THE STUNNING GROUNDS AT ROSEDOWN. DRIFTS OF KURUME 'SNOW' AZALEAS GROW IN LIGHT WOODLANDS FEATURING FLOWERING DOGWOOD. (ST. FRANCISVILLE)

THE SOUTHERN LIVE OAKS, QUERCUS VIRGINIANA, CONTRIBUTE WONDERFUL FORMS AND MOODS TO GARDENS. SPECIMENS GROWING IN THIS NEW ORLEANS PARK ARE MORE THAN 250 YEARS OLD. (CITY PARK, NEW ORLEANS)

A CLASSIC
SCENE ALONG
THE MISSISSIPPI
CORRIDOR IS
THE SWEEP OF
AZALEAS UNDER
THE LIVE OAKS,
ACCOMPANIED BY
SHADE-TOLERANT
PLANTS SUCH AS
ASPIDISTRA,
FERNS, AND
OTHER FOLIAGE
PLANTS. (TEZCUCO
PLANTATION,
BURNSIDE)

HANGING BASKETS AND WINDOWBOXES ARE TYPICAL OF THE MANY GALLERIES IN THE FRENCH QUARTER OF NEW ORLEANS.

MERCURY PASSING A MESSAGE TO SATYR. (RURAL LIFE MUSEUM, BATON ROUGE)

has almost every type of plant life thriving. Flowering seasons overlap and there are few days of the year when the city is without splendid color. Here the landscapes are full of exciting discoveries where elegance and sophistication create a special mood for outdoor living. Garden embellishment with pots, sculpture, water features, and other accessories further enriches the milieu.

*T*he New Orleans courtyard garden is small and self-contained, full of anticipation with tantalizing views, and crammed with lots of details. Gardening is practiced behind the rows of tightly packed houses, in the manner that other historic U.S. cities like Charleston, South Carolina, and Savannah, Georgia, experienced earlier. Unlike in Charleston where visitors have fairly open views into the gardens, in New Orleans the cityscape involves more closed and cloistered outdoor spaces—a fascinating world of patios with peepholes, lacy iron grilles, balconies and gates, through which agreeable snippets of gardens are eagerly gathered up by gardening enthusiasts. The picture is never complete since much is left to the imagination.

In the French Quarter (*Vieux Carré*) of New Orleans, with its eighteenth- and nineteenth-century buildings, there can be no such luxury as alleyways down the sides of buildings, or the breezeways typical of Charleston houses, which are orientated to allow sea breezes to waft between the houses. Instead, closed courtyard gardens have become a beloved hallmark of New Orleans.

The enclosed spaces are richly worked, each a complete garden entity. They are made to be appreciated from within. Surprises are sometimes designed to be arresting immediately upon entry, making intensely private and secret the eagerly awaited privileges of the interior garden experience. The setting is a perfect foil for some of the most exciting street life of any city in

LUSH, TROPICAL PLANTINGS ARE ENCLOSED BY A HEAVY ARBOR THAT SERVES AS AN EXTENSION OF THIS NEW ORLEANS GARDEN DISTRICT HOUSE. (HAYNE, NEW ORLEANS)

MANY SMALLER GARDENS HAVE COURTYARDS— AND WATER. AS A FEATURED ELEMENT, WATER PROVIDES SOME RELIEF FROM THE INTENSE SUMMER HEAT. (FRIERSON, NEW ORLEANS)

THE RICHNESS AND FULLNESS OF A GARDEN IN THE HEART OF THE GARDEN DISTRICT IN NEW ORLEANS, WITH ALLAMANDA AND PLUMBAGO GROWING AGAINST THE WALLS AND ROSES IN THE FOREGROUND. (STRACHAN)

the world. Gardens supply peace and solitude in counterpoint to the hustle of the streets.

Another equally important part of historic New Orleans for gardening is the "Garden District," which has some of the finest private gardens of any U.S. city. Built in the early 1800s, this section has gardens of considerably greater size than in the French Quarter. When traveling by trolley car along famous St. Charles Avenue or strolling through the area, there is a great air of botanical freshness and maturity. The best way to capture the flavor of the district is as a pedestrian.

On the plantations, space takes on a whole new significance. In complete contrast to the courtyard gardens of New Orleans where space is at a premium, plantation owners had as much as they cared to cut from the local wilderness—forests and cypress swamps. Their plantation homes nestled under mighty

LIVE OAK SPRAWLS ABOVE MAGNOLIA MOUND, WHICH IS POSITIONED ON A NATURAL LEVEE OF THE MISSISSIPPI RIVER. (BATON ROUGE)

*SITTING PROUDLY
ATOP A HILL IN
NATCHEZ, THE
ELEGANT STANTON
HALL, HEADQUARTERS
OF THE PILGRIMAGE
GARDEN CLUB, IS
SEEN THROUGH
A SPRINGTIME
FILIGREE OF
SPIREA, CAMELLIAS,
AND THE FOLIAGE
OF LIVE OAKS.*

*THE GOLDEN
AGE OF GARDENING
IN THE MIDDLE
OF THE LAST
CENTURY STILL
RESONATES IN
GARDENS ALONG
THE MISSISSIPPI.
IN THE SPIRIT OF
SOUTHERN
GARDENERS, THE
PRESENT OWNERS
OF AFTON
VILLA PURCHASED
THIS STONE-
CARVED STATUE,
"HOSPITALITY,"
IN ITALY.*

live oaks against a backdrop of sugar cane and cotton. The graceful limbs of the master oaks gave a languid air, but these were all working plantations, around which gardens evolved.

An account of the gardens of the lower Mississippi will inevitably be influenced by the architecture of the classical plantation houses that dominate these gardens. But the focus of this book is on the landscapes. Many plantation homes did not have highly acclaimed gardens reflecting a distinctive period style or ambience; some gardens were feeble, at best. On the other hand, large plantation mansions were often situated within beautiful grounds which themselves contributed a romantic spirit and character that still prevail today.

During and after the Civil War, many of the houses and gardens were left in a terrible state of neglect with only minimum maintenance for decades. Early gardens deteriorated rapidly. Uncontrollable growth took over the sites. Building materials disintegrated due to the abundance of moisture and heavy, unrestrained plant growth. Most of the fine sculpture and other garden embellishments were taken from the grounds.

In recent decades, however, new owners with enthusiasm and special vision for these historic places have given their properties new life. Large-scale renewal of the houses and grounds has taken place. While not constituting "restoration" in the classical definition of the term, adaptive reuse of these sites is providing enchanting home and gardens and adding immeasurable life and new pleasures to the once forgotten and nearly derelict places.

*L*arge by most gardening standards, plantation gardens were designed around the stately homes to offer extended views from the verandas down the oak avenues. Spaces are more open, allowing freedom to experience an expanded landscape well beyond the confines of the designated garden proper. Here there is a more casual, laid-back approach to gardening. The large parklike grounds with their informal plantings of mature trees and large shrub masses convey a mood totally different from that in town gardens. Many of these homes are close to their lifeblood, the old Mississippi River.

It is implicit in the study of plantation homes and gardens that they are a product of their working history. Many slaves and other workers lived on the property and kept it functioning. In essence, the first plantation gardens were like small, self-contained villages with routine work required for the operations of the complex. Indeed, on some plantations, relatives of the original owners still share the grounds with relatives of the original slaves who worked there.

Today, the garden buildings continue to play important roles in the overall settings. Many essential plantation activities took place in separate buildings such as the detached kitchen, milk shed, doctor's office, grist mill, carriage house, and overseer's quarters. Other buildings occupying important positions in the overall landscape scheme housed utility functions: the tool house, potting shed, and greenhouse; and the outside privy. At one time there were hundreds of plantation sites that included support buildings, but today few still have the entire complex intact.

Running a plantation garden was perhaps analogous to life on fine country estates in England and France, where in early times the household enjoyed the services of a host of gardeners. For example, Mrs. Wilmott of Warley Place in Essex (east of London) employed about two hundred gardeners in her three gardens, located in England, Italy, and Switzerland. In the Old World, it was the norm for centuries to establish gardens using lots of labor. The situation had not changed for two thousand years; Pliny the Younger had five hundred slave-gardeners dispersed around his three gardens; one in Rome, one in Tuscany, and the third on the coast at Ostia.

*T*oday, the views through century-old trees into the countryside beyond remind us of the naturalistic landscaped views planned by the famous English designers, "Capability" Brown and Humphry Repton, although southern gardens are somewhat thicker in vegetation now than 150 years ago when there were several thousand acres of cleared agricultural land around them. But the spirit of this riverside landscape lives on: boats' masts silently pass the end of the plantation *allées*—a time-warp of

SET BEHIND A DEFENSIVE BARRICADE OF SPLIT CYPRESS PICKETS, THIS TRADITIONAL WORKERS' COTTAGE WOULD HAVE HAD ITS OWN KITCHEN GARDEN. STEELE BURDEN RESCUED MANY OLD PICKETS FROM PLANTATION SITES ALONG THE RIVER. (RURAL LIFE MUSEUM)

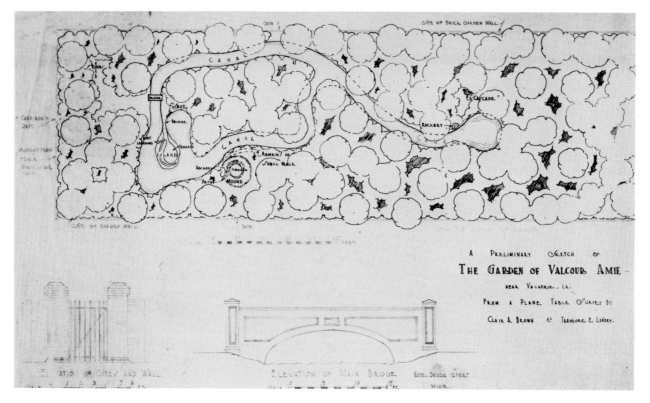

A RECONSTRUCTED PLAN OF THE EARLY-NINETEENTH-CENTURY LOUISIANA PLANTATION GARDEN, VALCOUR AIME, BY DR. CLAIR BROWN AND THEODORE E. LANDRY, WHO RESEARCHED THE SITE AND MADE A PLANE TABLE SURVEY IN 1941. ALTHOUGH IN RUINS TODAY, LOUISIANA'S "LITTLE VERSAILLES," OWNED BY THE SOUTH'S REPUTEDLY RICHEST PLANTER, CONTAINED MANY EXOTIC PLANTS IMPORTED FROM ALL OVER THE WORLD. (THEODORE E. LANDRY COLLECTION, LOUISIANA STATE UNIVERSITY LIBRARY)

yesterday still to be experienced from the galleries and belvederes of the plantation houses.

The allusion to the European park scene was not fortuitous, for it was a product of the diverse origins of the people in Louisiana and Mississippi. People from Italy, Germany, England, Spain and the Netherlands left their mark. Wealthy planters visited England and Europe frequently and kept alive the influence of their ancestry. On trips abroad, the landowners were heavily influenced by European garden layout, and they savored the formal geometric parterres as well as the more informal, naturalistic country and cottage garden designs. Antique garden embellishments poured in from Europe, especially expensive statuary and garden furniture, as well as exotic plants.

Rosedown, near St. Francisville, is a prime example of the European gardening genre which has been carefully preserved, capturing the spirit of the area near Baton Rouge in the first two decades of the 1800s.

The French gardening connection took hold in New Orleans—the gateway to the Mississippi and its plantations—and remains strong today. The French Quarter, by courtesy of its tightly knit community, developed its own special style, significantly different from the styles in France. To the north, people

CAPTURING THE CHARM AND MAGIC OF SPRINGTIME IN A MAGNIFICENTLY RESTORED PLANTATION GARDEN, THE WISTERIA AND AZALEAS EMBELLISH THIS PARTERRE GARDEN AT ROSEDOWN. (ST. FRANCISVILLE)

arrived overland by way of the Natchez Trace, an old trading route, and then settled on the precarious banks of the Mississippi River. Most of the plantations were in place prior to the 1850s.

Despite the diverse origins of the settlers, a common style of plantation garden evolved. Major constraints were the hot weather, relatively wet soils, and the need for shade, and the key factor facilitating rapid garden development was abundant slave labor. If New Orleans gardens were for quiet contemplation and absorbing the garden richness from within, those of the plantations had an extra ingredient; supplying grandeur in the views of and from the house. One typical plantation house that has its original layout intact is Oak Alley. The house is square, like most plantation homes, with one side facing the *allée* to the river, one overlooking a parterre, another viewing an English parklike scene through live oaks, and the back of the house opening to the support buildings.

Plantation owners enjoyed indulging in aristocratic, even snobbish, ventures. Building a grand Greek Revival house with an

ONCE AN ACTIVE SUGAR PLANTATION, OAK ALLEY (BON SÉJOUR) AND ITS GARDENS ARE AMONG LOUISIANA'S TREASURES. THE LARGE KETTLES WERE USED FOR MAKING SUGAR; TODAY THEY ARE PLACED AROUND THE GARDEN AS EMBELLISHMENTS. (VACHERIE)

equally imposing garden underscored a planter's status in the community. As gardening became *de rigueur*, larger and more pretentious developments emerged. Increasingly, visits to the renowned Old World gardens as well as contacts with the Eastern establishment influenced the size and scope of the landscape operations. It was viewed as the duty of a plantation owner to maintain a fine garden around the house.

Much of the foundation plant material used in plantation gardens is still present. In the face of neglect, there was heavy crowding because of the warm climate. But a surprising number of good performers persisted, forming masses of entangled junglelike growth—only to be rediscovered and reclaimed during the past three decades. Some of these faithful plants are now eagerly sought in old cemeteries, farm houses, center city gardens, and abandoned plantation sites. They are being reinstated as favored "period" plants for historic interpretations, and also as dependable performers in contemporary gardens. The long, tedious, and expensive process of reclaiming old gardens and plants is ongoing.

With new vision and a special enthusiasm for the places— and with increasing revenues, associated with a more prosperous economy and changed ownership—landscape renewal has evolved to a point of considerable acclaim. Predictably, attention to the affairs of the gardens has come about much more slowly than house restoration. Gardening renewal generally came after

BURSTING WITH CHARACTERISTIC ENERGY, THE SNOWY WHITE AZALEAS BURGEON AT THE GARDEN GATE AND MAKE A CHARMING FOIL AGAINST THE STATELY PARSONAGE IN NATCHEZ.

the house restoration work and the furnishing. Serious activity really began in the 1950s with work progressing until the present. The finery and rich garden history locked up in these places is only now seeing its new lease on life.

There is considerable contrast between plantations that have been lovingly restored with extensive financial investment, and those that have drifted along to the present in their own serene manner. Both are splendiferous. The first kind are notable for their beautiful beds and borders, with a strong emphasis on formal style as defined by architectural structures and associated paths, walls, water, and other features, while the second are recognized and featured here because of their romantic country style, definitely informal. Both express a distinctive quality and mood.

While one may take nostalgic pleasure in a garden style that matched the gracious aspects of the days of carriages and ladies in hooped skirts, inevitably, the pendulum has swung away from all that. Today, many people favor more casual, lower-maintenance gardens. Budgets are seldom equal to pursuing gardens of the size and scope of yesteryear. Instead, the naturalistic style has prospered, benefiting gardening enthusiasts who wish to respond to the rising interest in indigenous plant species. As habits change due to the rapid growth of plants, the mood of gardens also evolves. Swathes of shade-loving groundcover plants are now having their own renaissance. An enthusiasm for the "wilder," more natural garden style is emerging as mini-gardens within larger gardens, such as the Wild Garden at Longue Vue (New Orleans) and the small bog garden at Melrose (Natchez).

AERIAL VIEW OF FORMAL GARDEN, CEMETERY, AND GROUNDS AT AFTON VILLA. (ST. FRANCISVILLE)

Punctuation

Walls, Fences, Gates and Verandas

I entered the front yard—

a green level, shaded with the

relics of a forest—the live oak,

sycamore, and gum trees—

through a narrow wicket in a

whitewashed paling, the most common

fence around southern dwellings.

Joseph Holt Ingraham • 1835

*T*he division of the land along the banks of the Mississippi River during the late eighteenth century followed a very formal pattern of straight fences perpendicular to the river. Joseph Ingraham described the system in his 1835 book, *The South-West By a Yankee*: "Plantations along the river extend from the levee to the swamps in the rear; the distance across the belt of land being, from the irregular encroachment of the marshes, from one to two or three miles." The geometrical pattern of long rectangles and irregular trapeze shapes, repeated hundreds of times, is highlighted on maps of the plantation properties.

Seen from the plantation homes, the fences served as a point of reference for land ownership, and often paralleled the live oak avenues leading to the river. The geometric outlines of the plantations have altered very little from original demarcation, although most land holdings today are only a fraction of the vast acreages of earlier times. The flatlands adjacent to the banks of the Mississippi were conducive to the unhindered run of fence posts, so that the topography helped to determine the patterns.

In *The Plantation South*, Katharine Jones cites the recollections of *London Times* writer William Howard Russell of his 1863 visit to Louisiana plantations, and his impressions upon arrival at Houmas House Plantation at Burnside across the river from Donaldsonville:

I ascended the bank, and across the road, directly in front, appeared a carriage gateway and wickets of wood, painted white, in a line of park palings of the same material, which extended up and down the road as far as the eye could see, and guarded wide-spread fields of maize and sugar-cane. An avenue lined with trees, with branches close set, drooping and overarching a walk paved with red brick, led to the house, the porch of which was visible at the extremity of the lawn, with clustering flowers, rose, jessamine, and creepers clinging to the pillars, supporting the veranda. The view from the belvedere on the roof was one of the most striking of its kind in the world.

There is no doubt that fences here often serve as an esthetic backdrop, providing vertical contrast to the flat landscape.

*F*encing and garden gates in the plantation or country garden also serve several other purposes. As Russell noted in 1863: "If an English agriculturist could see six thousand acres of the finest land in one field, unbroken by hedge or boundary, and covered with the most magnificent crops of tasseling Indian corn and sprouting sugarcane, as level as a billard table, he would surely doubt his senses. But here is literally such a sight—six thousand acres." With such vast acreage, one can readily see the need to define a particular site at a reduced scale for gardening pleasures.

In addition, fences provided protection for the garden from the farm animals, as well as aggressive wild animals. In Martha Turnbull's nineteenth-century diary of her nearly sixty years of gardening at Rosedown Plantation (St. Francisville), she noted: "Poultry bad on my roses . . . The hogs are doing great damage up

'SIMPLICITY' ROSES, BACKED BY A CONTEMPORARY PICKET FENCE, ARE FEATURED IN THIS SMALL COTTAGE GARDEN IN NATCHEZ.

EXAMPLE OF EARLY "VIRGINIA" OR "SNAKE" SPLIT-RAIL PLANTATION FENCE ATOP BLUFF IN NATCHEZ OVERLOOKING THE MISSISSIPPI. IN THE COLONIAL PERIOD, THE NUMBER OF RAILS USED COULD VARY FROM THREE TO NINE DEPENDING ON THE SECURITY NEEDED FROM INTRUDING ANIMALS. (ROSALIE, NATCHEZ)

A TRADITIONAL PICKET FENCE CONTAINS A RESTORED GARDEN. PICKETS MADE OF LOCAL SWAMP CYPRESS DO NOT READILY ROT. WHITEWASHING IS OF COMPARATIVELY RECENT ORIGIN—NOTWITHSTANDING MARK TWAIN'S FAMOUS PASSAGE WITH TOM SAWYER. (RURAL LIFE MUSEUM)

the Avenue & Garden generally—hogs rooting around Quince trees . . . & the young Japonicas continually."

Some fences were shaped in a zigzag pattern while other stock fences were made of post and horizontally laid timbers all pinned together into one impenetrable corral-type fence. Some of the authentic examples, such as the kitchen garden at Magnolia Mound (Baton Rouge) and Maison Chenal (Point Coupee Parish), have split cypress *pieux* (picket) arranged vertically as examples of the highly popular picket fence. The timber was usually the native swamp cypress cut from the surrounding land, and was generally unpainted. Only on the wealthier plantations were the pickets painted white, adding an extra visual richness to the scene. At Rosedown, Martha Turnbull noted in August 1838: "It took 6 men 4 days to do our fence—& 4 barrels lime unslacked." Much later, in January 1875, her diary entry gives a clue to the size and scope of fence building: "I had 14 thousand rails split—& they have made a large quantity of fence . . . All working diligently at the fences."

Today the fence rows remain as legal boundaries, occasionally supplemented by a vigorous growth of volunteer plants seeded by birds, and these demarcations represent an important element on the plantation sites today. Controlling the limits of a space by providing an edge immediately sets boundaries in which gardens can be created.

Unlike in the rural landscape, in New Orleans, where demand on the land has always been very keen, fences and walls take on a completely different role. In early days walls and fences were used primarily for security; but today garden enclosures are symbols of intimacy and privacy as well. They also muffle sounds and obscure views both from within and from the outside. Barriers five to seven feet high of clipped evergreens, brick, wood, or a combination of several materials form the outdoor rooms in which some of our most cherished gardening experiences take place. Here designers work to create intimate enclaves of *treillage* and lattices in place of fences, and these give the gardens extra character.

There is always the age-old concern of simultaneously attempting to provide both intimacy in these small spaces and yet also a sense of spaciousness, so that the outdoor areas will not appear too confining. For this one needs careful blending of plants and "hardscape" construction materials. Such management practices as pruning of the plants also play an important role in the final spirit of the place. The narrow lots of New Orleans gardens, squeezed in between the cheek-by-jowl houses, necessarily encouraged development of the enclosed or secret garden sanctuaries.

Cramped living conditions in small tenements spilling into utilitarian courts (similar in appearance to the silk-weavers' garrets in London or Lyon) must have been horrendous to live in by today's standards—a far cry from the cozy courtyard gardens where sensitive restoration has now created highly appealing nooks.

*T*he French courtyard gardens, as expressed in New Orleans, are perhaps better perfected than many in Paris, Nice, and Marseilles. New Orleans has the advantage in its French Quarter

SIMPLICITY IN DESIGN, PLANTINGS, AND EMBELLISHMENT: THIS GARDEN WALL IN THE HEART OF NEW ORLEANS SHOWS OFF A BEAUTIFUL WALL POT WITH IVY AND STAGHORN FERN. (MELTON AND SCALIA)

VERTICAL SCREENING AND PRUNING AT ITS BEST: SOUTHERN MAGNOLIA IS USED WITH GREAT ORIGINALITY TO FORM A TWELVE- TO FIFTEEN-FOOT HEDGEROW. INTEGRATED INTO THE FLOWING BED ARE AZALEAS, CITRUS, DECIDUOUS MAGNOLIAS, AND MONDO GROUNDCOVER. (HINES, METAIRE)

of some fine architecture that makes a characterful backdrop for Riviera gardens. Contemporary architecture cannot possibly recreate the atmosphere and charm of New Orleans with its wrought iron balconies and rich brickwork.

Traditional materials in the region used for enclosures include brick, stuccoed concrete block, wood, and iron work. Walls help to provide a strong linkage to architectural styles and building materials. In addition, plants closely placed and clipped can provide the effect of a solid, impenetrable barrier. Brick is probably the most popular material because it is readily available and easily blended with the architecture. Detailing varies tremendously from simple brick and mortar to intricate capstone and coping, punctuated with special textured surfaces and adorned with gardening embellishment. In many cases bricks for stuccoed and painted columns were made on site by slaves, and the original molds still exist on some plantations, such as Parlange (New Roads).

Walls are a wonderful foil for plants. The surfaces moderate extremes in temperatures and form ideal microclimates and settings for such traditional favorites as the climbing roses, wisteria, Carolina jessamine, allamanda, and rosa de Montana. By absorbing sunlight, the walls stay warmer for longer than exposed sites in winter and heat up earlier in spring, thus extending the growing season by several weeks. Walls often serve as barriers to chilling winds, and moderate the environment sufficiently to allow more tender plants to escape winter freezes. On the other hand, walls can also protect plants from harsh direct sun at critical times of day during summer. Water seeps into the soil along the foundations, allowing plants to thrive in what might otherwise be droughty conditions. Some plants, like clematis, dogwood, hydrangea, camellias, and ferns, do especially well where their roots are shaded during the hottest time of the day.

INSPIRED BY THE GARDEN OF THE ALHAMBRA IN SOUTHERN SPAIN, THIS WALL CASCADE GIVES A REFRESHING SOURCE OF WATER SOUNDS IN AN OTHERWISE FORMAL GARDEN. (LONGUE VUE GARDENS)

THE OPEN IRONWORK FENCING REVEALS RATHER THAN HIDES THIS RICH GARDEN ENCLAVE, FESTOONED WITH A VIGOROUS MAPLE VINE. NOTE THE DECORATIVE SUGAR KETTLE FEATURED IN THE ADJOINING GARDEN. (MISTLETOE, NATCHEZ)

*B*rick and concrete walls and other permanent surfaces provide an ideal location for espaliers (the name comes from an old Italian word, *spalla*, which means shoulder supports or the "shouldering" of a plant). For both decorative purposes and as a means of conserving space, this controlled pruning technique forces plants to grow only in a flat plane against a designated surface like a wall or other flat support structure. Even large-growing fruiting plants like pear, apple, fig, loquat, and citrus can thus be persuaded to grow in extremely narrow spaces. Many flowering shrubs, like banana shrub, sweet olive, sasanqua, camellia, or althea, perform equally well trained against a wall. For some of the less cold-hardy plants like citrus, loquat, and plumbago, which are susceptible to freezes, south-facing walls provide some protection and insulation from damaging temperatures. There are many methods of pruning plants to create different shapes or natural wall coverings.

As walls age and become weathered with cracks and crevices, and mortar is lost between bricks, mosses, lichens, and ferns find a perfect haven. They give a mature appearance to any garden. (The aging process can be hastened—the surface made more suitable for these small native species—by applying water-soluble fertilizer to the wall or rubbing on yoghurt, buttermilk, or compost leachate.) Weathered walls can be an attractive growing environment for a large number of native and introduced wall-clinging species.

A host of introduced and naturally occuring vines with clinging roots will invade a wall if given a chance. These include Virginia creeper, trumpet creeper, and the introduced species English ivy, fig vine, and the highly aggressive cat's claw vine. Controlled as a tracery of foliage, they can provide a wonderful softening element to walls and fences. Soft, porous brick, which sustains a high moisture content, provides the most attractive surface for plants.

"Vertical gardening" is a popular practice in which the wall surfaces become an integral part of the design palette. New opportunities and challenges are created by introducing a wider assortment of interesting plants to the garden setting. In the limited spaces associated with the older courtyards and contemporary townhouse gardens, it pays to focus on plant species that grow well either attached to the surfaces or as ramblers using walls and fences for vertical support.

*M*ost plants can grow and thrive in an amazingly small volume of soil. Their growth rate and ultimate height and spread may be reduced by a restricted root system, but this in turn may adapt them better for the smaller spaces. Pockets of deep soil can provide for a surprisingly large number of plants, although more frequent watering and feeding may be required than for plants growing under more generous conditions.

The garden gate is always inviting, especially one that is ajar. At that magic point of entry, curiosity is aroused and anticipation of what lies beyond colors the overall garden experience. Gates are symbols of both control and welcome and there can often be a struggle between the emanations of welcome and those of privacy. Gates are sometimes formidable and constructed of solid materials, shutting out peering eyes from the merest hint of secrets that lie within. For other situations, gates of wrought iron or other more open materials form a barrier and create a certain

LICHENS THRIVE ON THE GATE AND ALONG THE FENCE OF THIS PLANTATION GARDEN, DUE TO THE SHADY AND COOL ENVIRONMENT CREATED BY THE MIGHTY LIVE OAKS. (ALMA PLANTATION, LAKELAND)

BLOSSOMING WITH EFFERVESCENT EXUBERANCE, A LADY BANKSIA ROSE SCRAMBLES OVER A FENCE WITH ENORMOUS ARCHING CANES.

sense of wonder, but do not impede the view totally. To further heighten anticipation, grilles, peepholes and other windowlike openings may provide glimpses into gardens. These allow one to become prepared for the fuller experience that gradually unfolds upon entry. In enclosed city gardens, gates and doors in the wall are often the point of entry for the entire living complex, since the garden itself may be an integral extension of the house.

The concept of compartmentalizing gardens was pioneered by the English (Jekyll and Lutyens most famously) primarily to shut out the wind, and to form a better microclimate for plants. Places like Hidcote (Gloucestershire) and Sissinghurst (Kent) are classic examples of compartmentalizing gardens. Sissinghurst, according to its designer, Vita Sackville-West, is a "garden with all its separate rooms and sub-sections...must be a garden of seasonal features through the year." It is intrigue and curiosity that drive people to venture on through a gate into another compartment garden, as at Great Dixter, a garden with eighteen compartments and the home of plantsman and garden writer Christopher Lloyd in Sussex, England.

*I*n many of the gardens along the Mississippi River, plantings in the form of hedgerows were used to create compartments, as seen at Rosedown, Afton Villa, Houmas House, and at many homes within the town of Natchez. Plantings in the form of living hedges may be tall and restrictive but include low areas to reveal the treasures of the next garden section. From these controlled spaces the vistor often gets glimpses of the borrowed scenery well beyond the confines of the featured garden or even the property.

However, a more open, casual, informal approach to compartmentalizing in the plantation garden is much more fitting to the overall ambience and dignity of the place. In colonial days, plants such as privet, Banksia and Cherokee and other roses, mock orange, holly, Cape jasmine, and cherry laurel were used as *au naturel* barriers to separate gardens into clearly defined sectors. Martha Turnbull refers to trimming a couple of the more unusual hedges in her diary: "Trimmed down the wild peach hedge very low...all hedges cliped...myrtle hedge in full bloom." Hedges were not everywhere apparent in the early days, however. Ingraham noted in 1835 after visiting New Orleans and Natchez:

> I noticed within the fence a young hedge, which, with an unparalleled innovation upon the prescriptive right of twisted fences, had recently been planted to supersede them. In a country where the "Chickasaw rose," which is a beautiful hedge thorn, grows so luxuriantly, it is worthy of remark that the culture of the hedge, so ornamental and useful as a field-fence, is altogether neglected.

Gates and archways are useful garden embellishments and become special "nodes" or intersections in the general garden

MAXIMIZING THE VALUE OF A BRICK WALL, CONTAINERS OF WHITE BEGONIAS ARE EXHIBITED IN THIS NEW ORLEANS GARDEN. (TULLIS, NEW ORLEANS)

plan. Changes in moods and styles often take place here. Being led from one part to another through a sequence of "rooms" can be pleasant and intriguing. The element of surprise at every node is a classical ploy long practiced in the Orient. In Chinese and Japanese gardens the juxtaposition of concealment and revelation was a form used to great advantage to make a site appear much larger than it really was. The same techniques are employed in our gardens today.

Galleries and verandas on some or all sides of a house play an essential role in garden design, as from elevated positions offering wonderful views. Broad porches also provide shade to the walls and windows and give a comfortable space for outdoor living. Periodic flooding and the hot, humid climate in the low Delta country necessitated raised upper-story living quarters. Indeed, the perspective of many a fine plantation home has been planned to accommodate the esthetics best from on high. Mid-

Seven generations of planters have sat on this gallery enjoying the grounds. The gentle quivering of the banana leaves reaches up to the second floor. (Parlange Plantation, New Roads)

nineteenth-century Houmas House, Rosedown, San Francisco, Parlange, Nottoway as well as estates such as Longue Vue (New Orleans) in the twentieth century utilized the same architectural technique.

At Longue Vue the loggia—that part of the gallery so placed as to see along the length of the main garden *allée*—is brilliantly executed. Although Longue Vue is strongly influenced from Granada in Spain, the idea of having a garden design specifically for an overview had long been a major feature of fine French and Italian gardens. Many French *château* gardens have spectacular overviews, such as Château Villandry in the Loire Valley and in many of the Italian and French Riviera gardens

where topography lends itself to views across terraces tumbling down hillsides to the sea.

Gardens like these were often designed with symbolistic patterns and colors to be viewed from above; the gardens were not specifically planned for strolling, but for more distant visual enjoyment. Though there is nothing quite so spectacular along the flat Mississippi River corridor, the same design techniques have been employed to take the best advantage of pleasant scenes of inviting countryside seen through an open structure of live oaks.

Some of these scenes, such as the gently undulating ground of Rosalie or the meandering open spaces at Oak Alley and

Melrose (Natchez), are reminiscent of the English countryside as manicured by "Capability" Brown. This effect is repeated many times where there are no formal gardens, and the grounds have been cleaned of undergrowth to emphasize grand parklike tree plantings as seen at many of the Natchez, St. Francisville, and River Road homes. The effect is very English in style and mood— one might expect to see a herd of deer or cattle grazing.

Galleries succeed brilliantly in easing the transition between house and garden in this climate. In Europe one might strive to make the garden "another room of the house," but the effort is likely to be less successful since doors are usually required to shut out the elements. But in Louisiana and Mississippi, as else-

DIVISION BETWEEN THE HOUSE AND GARDEN IS MODERATED BY THE OPEN GALLERY AND STAIRS. (THE BURN, NATCHEZ)

FRONT AND REAR, THE GALLERY STAIRS PROVIDE AN IMPORTANT LINK TO THE GARDEN. (LIVE OAK PLANTATION, WEYANOKE)

where in the South, the amiable climate allows a strong bond between interior and exterior. Glass from floor to ceiling is used extensively in windows and doors. In fact, doors and windows are interchangeable in many homes. Before air conditioning, verandas and galleries were places to savor any breeze, or to sip something cool while relaxing in a rocking chair. Even in modest homes the indoor-outdoor interface was well developed. Shotgun houses and dog-trot cabins allowed the air to pass straight through the buildings, so that the garden space actually flowed through the house from one side to the other, a quality very few houses outside the South can boast.

From galleries an ideal overview of the estate can be appreciated. Not only does the flow of space into the garden begin to make sense from this vantage point—along the *allée* to the river, or across the fences to the fields—but one has the feeling of already being in the garden, or being a part of it, from the sanctuary of this intermediate viewing stage. When fragrances from highly scented plants such as sweet olive (*Osmanthus fragrans*), banana shrub (*Michelia figo*), and magnolia (*Magnolia grandiflora*) are wafting your way, the olfactory and visual effect is memorable and enveloping.

3

Pigeonniers and their Kin

In a grand Paris restaurant I once found pigeons

the most expensive dish on the menu. But it was, of course,

a pigeonneau or Bordeaux pigeon—what we call a squab—

young, plump and broad-breasted, barely airborne yet

and especially reared for the table. For centuries, all

the great houses of Europe had their dovecotes—

you can see them still at Château Mouton Rothschild.

MARGARET COSTA
FOUR SEASONS COOKERY BOOK • 1976

No accent in the plantation gardens of Louisiana and Mississippi is as prominent or distinctive as their *pigeonniers* and *garçonnières*. They are follies of extravagant proportions— grand embellishments that make bold statements, and often painted white to emphasize them further. They are matchless in their variety and flamboyant contributions to their settings.

Besides being symbols of status and of liberty, and the source of meat viewed as a delicacy, the *pigeonniers*, of course, contained birds, which gave the landscape an appealing animation. For enthusiasts who like to have creatures in the garden (and among their antecedents we must number the Romans, the gardeners of Renaissance Italy, and even Henry VIII with his petrified griffons on plinths) the *pigeonnier* is simply a glorified birdhouse, dressed up in the best finery and elevated to a success story in garden embellishment.

Pigeonniers along the Mississippi corridor reflect a very strong French influence. There are so many in some regions of France, especially the north, that near Le Havre there is now a tourist route called *Route des Colombières* ("way of the doves") in the Cauchois area of Normandy. The custom of eating squabs, fledgeling chicks taken from the nest, had developed because it was a good deal more convenient a method of obtaining game birds than by relying on hunting.

In England and Europe in medieval times, pigeon-rearing went on in the towers of castles. The late fourteenth-century moated Bodiam Castle (Kent) has a round tower complete with holes especially for pigeons. A fifteenth-century dovecote at Athelhampton has a thousand nesting holes. A large circular one at Rousham House (Oxfordshire) and the ancient pigeon-house at Cotehele in Cornwall were restored in 1962 by the National Trust.

When times became a little more secure for living in manors without fortifications, the dovecote, as it was known in England, became an integral part of the garden, as essential to the country house complex as the cow sheds and poultry houses. Historic dovecotes include those at the fourteenth-century Kinwarton (Warwickshire), the medieval Charleston manor (Sussex), and the fifteenth-century example at Wilminton (Devon). Usually they are round or octagonal, with conical roofs. Some still have resident pigeons.

According to the *Dictionary of Architecture and Building*, in France, "The maintenance by the lord of the manor of a great number of pigeons which fed freely on the fields of his tenants was one of the crying abuses of the feudal system." The peasants hated having the aristocratic pigeons grow fat on their cabbages, especially if a flock of 2,000 landed in their kitchen gardens. The right to have a *pigeonnier* was among the

IN COMPLETE HARMONY WITH ITS SURROUNDINGS, THIS PIGEONNIER IS CONSTRUCTED WITH OVERLAPPING CYPRESS TIMBERS. IT SITS AMID A COMPLEX OF BUILDINGS ON THE GROUNDS OF THIS LOUISIANA CREOLE GARDEN. (HOLDEN, CHENAL)

OLD TERRACOTTA POTS CREATE A WONDERFUL FOREGROUND FOR THE VIEW THROUGH THE LIVE OAKS TO THE ORIGINAL PIGEONNIER; A BEAUTIFUL SETTING "EXQUISITELY GRATIFYING IN TASTE AND SCENT," TO QUOTE ONE DESCRIPTION OF AMBROSIA PLANTATION, ST. FRANCISVILLE.

demands in the great uprising of the French people—the French Revolution.

Prior to this, the *pigeonnier* was fundamental to the overall plan of the French estate, and symbolized one's membership in the aristocracy. *Pigeonniers* ranged in size from modest proportions (thirty to forty-five feet in Midi-Pyrennes) to much larger structures of grandiose design, attached to the main house. After the Revolution, by August 1789, the peasants of France were allowed for the first time to have their own *pigeonniers*. Pigeon-lofts blossomed everywhere, constructed hurriedly from simple materials readily at hand, and thus the *pigeonnier* acquired a more rustic look.

TUCKED AWAY IN THE CORNER OF A WOODLAND GARDEN, THIS CONTEMPORARY HEXAGONAL PIGEONNIER, OR PAVILION, HAS AN INTERESTING ARRANGEMENT OF FLIGHT HOLES. LONGUE VUE GARDEN, NEW ORLEANS.

THE VIEW OF THE GARDEN TAKEN BY THEODORE LANDRY IN 1963, SHOWING HOUMAS HOUSE'S PARTERRE FLANKED BY TWO PIGEONNIERS. (THEODORE E. LANDRY COLLECTION, LOUISIANA STATE UNIVERSITY)

In Louisiana and Mississippi the *pigeonnier* has remained modest in size, and usually separate from the house. But the fact that the *pigeonnier* has fine architectural detail has promoted it to the position of centerpiece in many plantation gardens. Indeed, the status symbol of having a fine pair of *pigeonniers* under the live oaks outside a plantation house mirrors the history of their role in France. In the early gardens, construction of *pigeonniers* still symbolized affluence and wealth, and provided a bold statement about who was in charge. A variation of the feudal system persisted along the banks of the Mississippi well after 1789, and passersby were duly notified of the opulent lifestyle of plantation owners by these highly decorative embellishments.

One wonders how important was the raising of squabs, in light of the plentiful game and wildfowl along the swamps and forests of the Mississippi, when compared to the status of having pigeons in the garden. In France, pigeons would have grown fat from feeding on grain after the harvest, but in Louisiana and Mississippi there would have been no leavings for pigeons after picking cotton or cutting sugar cane. Nevertheless, on some southern plantations the *pigeonnier* did supply meat. Papers from the Butler family of West Feliciana Parish, cited in the *Magnolia Mound Plantation Kitchen Book*, provide a recipe for preparing squab that was used during the first half of the nineteenth century (for a twentieth-century adaptation, use eight Cornish hens):

VIEWED THROUGH THE FOLIAGE OF TWO NATIVE PLANTS, THE SOUTHERN MAGNOLIA AND THE LIVE OAK, THE SQUARE PIGEONNIER AT MAGNOLIA MOUND LOOKS VERY MUCH AS IT MIGHT HAVE EARLY IN THE NINETEENTH CENTURY, WHEN THE PROPERTY WAS ENLARGED FROM A TYPICAL SETTLER'S COTTAGE. (BATON ROUGE)

A FRICASEY OF PIGEONS

Take 8 pigeons, new killed, cut them in small pieces and put them in a stew pan with a pint of claret and a pint of water. Season your pigeons with salt and pepper, a blade or two of mace, an onion, a bunch of sweet herbs, a good piece of butter just rolled in a very little flour; cover it close and let them stew until there is just enough for sauce, and then take out the onion and sweet herbs and beat the yolk of three eggs, grate half a nutmeg and with your spoon push the meat all to one side of the pan and the gravy to the other, and stir in the eggs; keep them stirring for fear of turning curds, and when the sauce is fine and thick shake all together, and then put them into the dish, pour the sauce over it, and ready some slices of bacon toasted and fried oysters, throw the oysters all over and lay the bacon.

The Magnolia Mound book also offers this insight: "Pigeons: There are various sorts—tame, wild, and wood pigeons. The tame were the most in use. Wild pigeons were tasty boiled or roasted, but not in fricasses or ragouts, as the flesh was considered too 'black.'"

The role of the *pigeonnier* slowly slipped from being a useful means of providing meat to being an important and decorative garden feature. Today most are in good repair, although few have any resident pigeons. The designs of American *pigeonniers* have been many and various, to a degree that some are unique.

The range of styles seen in Dominique Letellier's recent book on French *pigeonniers* which proliferated along the Mississippi River corridor are fabulous in their own way.

*T*he origin of *pigeonniers* goes back at least 2,000 years to the Romans. Pliny the Elder, for example wrote about the fine details of construction. The Persians, Greeks, and Egyptians also dabbled in pigeon-houses and what is known from these early periods is that the typical shape was round. Forms ranged from the stately sixteenth-century *pigeonniers* in Calvados in the north of France to the more typical rounded form—almost like a shepherd's hut—called a *pigeonnier-gariotte* in the south of France. None of the Mississippi River corridor *pigeonniers* show this influence, however.

Square, octagonal, and polygonal *pigeonniers* were frequently made in France and, as indicated, in England most were round or octagonal, but along the Mississippi square and hexagonal ones are the norm. Square or rectangular ones are found at Magnolia Mound, Ambrosia, Seven Oaks, Rosedown, and Maison Chenal, for example, and hexagonal ones at Parlange and Longue Vue. In the garden context, hexagonal *pigeonniers* are most interesting, but the rustic styles (as at Maison Chenal and Rosedown) seem more fitting, since they are of the same time frame as those built in rural France.

A FINE HEXAGONAL PIGEONNIER, ONE OF A PAIR, GRACES THE FRONT LAWN AT PARLANGE PLANTATION. NOW TASTEFULLY CONVERTED TO A PIED-À-TERRE, IT ASSUMES THE MODERN ROLE OF A GARÇONNIÈRE. LIKE THE PLANTATION HOUSE, THE PIGEONNIERS WERE BUILT BY SLAVE LABOR FROM BRICKS MADE ON THE PLANTATION, AND DATE FROM THE EARLY NINETEENTH CENTURY. (NEW ROADS)

As if to emphasize the role of the *pigeonnier* in the garden, American *pigeonniers* were never joined to the house. No plantation house had a "tower" designed for pigeons (*pigeonnier-tourelle*), or a loft for them above an entrance door, as in *pigeonnier-porche*, or a pigeon section in a granary (*pigeonnier-grenie*r), though at Dunleith the poultry house and pigeon coop combined does give a farmyard flavor of some historical note. Had Dunleith's castellations on the "tower" of the greenhouse been transferred to the *pigeonnier* as well, it might have reflected the castle-*pigeonnier* form. One *pigeonnier* style apparently absent from the Mississippi corridor is that on columns; this might have been appropriate because of floodwaters, but might also have detracted from the imposing style of the plantation house.

*A*s regards the finer detailing on *pigeonniers*, French forms seem to have been followed more precisely. The finishing touches at the top of the French *pigeonnier* (the *épis de faîtage*) were often made of pottery, metal, or of carved stone. The variation of *lucarnes* (attic windows), often rendered along the Mississippi corridor as belvederes set in roof space, are comparable.

If the function of *pigeonniers* in plantation gardens departed somewhat from their original purpose in Europe, the nature of *garçonnières* in the Mississippi River corridor departed

NOW CONVERTED TO A TEA HOUSE, THIS "CHICKEN COOP" TOPPED BY A DOVECOTE SERVED THE HOUSEHOLD AT DUNLEITH WITH FRESH MEAT AND SQUABS. (NATCHEZ)

even more from what the French considered a *garçonnière* to be. In the usual sense of the word, a *garçonnière* is a "bachelor pad," a flat for a bachelor. In Louisiana and Mississippi, a *garçonnière* was simply a place where boys old enough to play cards and wear long trousers were encouraged to go to get out of the house. As Robinson and Robinson describe in their work on early houses in the *Vieux Carré* of New Orleans,

> Toward the rear along one side of the courtyard was found the *garçonnière* or "boys" quarters. The building

THIS PART WOOD, PART RED BRICK GARÇONNIÈRE STANDS WELL BACK FROM THE ORIGINAL HOUSE, WHICH BURNED IN 1960. (GREENWOOD, ST. FRANCISVILLE)

SHELTERED BY THE
EXTRAORDINARY
LONG ARM OF A
MIGHTY LIVE
OAK (HOST TO A
COLONY OF WILD
HONEYBEES),
ONE OF TWO
GARCONNIÈRES
AT HOUMAS HOUSE.
CONSTRUCTED OF
BRICK AND PLASTER,
THE GARÇONNIÈRES
AT HOUMAS HOUSE
ARE AMONG THE
BEST PRESERVED OF
THE TRADITIONAL
BACHELOR'S
QUARTERS.
(BURNSIDE)

had one or two stories at different levels from the main house. Each story had a gallery, and little stair cases connected them. The *garçonnière* was sometimes used for extra guests, but primarily it was for the youngsters. Here they could come and go, or tear around without tracking mud on the best rugs or upsetting the best parlor furniture.

Garçonnières, as their name suggests, were strictly for the boys; girls were never given a free hand and were kept under strict control in the house and around the garden.

Some American *garçonnières*, however, reflected their origin more closely. In *The Plantation South* Katherine Jones quotes William Russell of the *London Times*, following his 1863 visit to Louisiana:

> I found...a few merchants from New Orleans in possession of the bachelors' house. The service performed by slaves and the order and regularity of the attendants were worthy of a well-regulated English mansion.

A third kind of structure in the Mississippi River corridor is also often a prominent garden feature, occupying a key position that rivals that of *pigeonniers* and *garçonnières*: the cistern. These tend to be taller and more heavily embellished than

THIS TRADITIONAL CISTERN AT SAN FRANCISCO PLANTATION STANDS AS A FINE GARDEN EMBELLISHMENT BESIDE THE PLANTATION HOUSE. (GARYVILLE)

THE GIANT WATER
CISTERN AT TEZCUCO
PLANTATION (BURNSIDE)
IS UNIQUE. THE
CISTERN SERVED NOT
ONLY AS A SOURCE
OF WATER FOR THE
HOUSEHOLD BUT
AS AN EMERGENCY
SOURCE OF WATER
IN CASE OF FIRE.
THE MAGNOLIA
MOUND
PLANTATION
KITCHEN BOOK
DESCRIBED, "THE
WATER WAGON
WAS FILLED FROM
THE CISTERN AND
PULLED TO THE
FIELD DAILY."

pigeonniers and garçonnières, and sometimes have ironwork and
trellis around the conical top. Cisterns were for storing the water
needed in the household—and for fighting fires—and were often
built in pairs. References in early writings indicate the importance
of having available water for the field hands and concern was often
voiced during periods of drought. In September 1893, diarist
Martha Turnbull noted that drought had rendered many cisterns
empty. Today most cisterns and wellhead structures are included

as part of garden embellishment. New Orleans courtyard gardens still contain old cisterns, below and above ground, used for water storage. The cistern in the center of the formal garden at Oakley is nearly thirty feet deep.

On the plantations, cisterns, *pigeonniers* and other garden embellishments were kept in immaculate order. A particularly fine example can be seen in an old print of Albania Plantation drawn in 1861 and figured in Paul Stahl's book on homes in the Teche country. It is a square, white-painted *pigeonnier* with a peaked roof finished in a finial, not unlike the one found today at Magnolia Mound in design and restoration.

Handsome examples of a paired *pigeonnier* and *garçonnière* stand on the front lawn at Parlange, square in shape and well preserved. The *garçonnière* has been converted to a fine *pied à terre*. Martha Turnbull's *pigeonnier* at Rosedown, seen across the garden pond, has a uniquely rustic look much improved by its reflection in the water. She makes several journal references to it, noting for example on April 18, 1891, "just cleaning Pigeon house and . . . 8 young."

THE OLD UNDERGROUND WATER CISTERN, WHICH SERVED THE HOUSEHOLD AT OAKLEY PLANTATION (ST. FRANCISVILLE), IS NOW THE FOCAL POINT OF THE FORMAL GARDEN.

THIS RUSTIC PIGEONNIER, SET ACROSS THE POND FROM THE HOUSE, MAKES AN ATTRACTIVE FOCAL POINT. THE ANIMATION OF THE PIGEONS REFLECTED IN THE WATER. MARTHA TURNBULL REFERS TO THIS PIGEON HOUSE AT LEAST TWICE IN HER DIARY, ONCE IN MAY 1890—"HANNA CLEANED PIGEON HOUSE"—AND IN MAY 1891—"JUST CLEANING PIGEON HOUSE AND 18 YOUNG ONES." (ROSEDOWN)

The *pigeonnier* at Ambrosia Plantation (St. Francisville) is unique, subtly painted in black and white so that from a distance it shows a huge black cross—perhaps coincidental, but it seems not. At Angelina Plantation (St. Charles Parish), built in 1852, a pair of decorated dovecotes once stood to the rear of the home, but have since been taken by the Mississippi. These picturesque hexagonal dovecotes were made of whitewash brick, and crowned with weather vanes. Other plantations which had *pigeonniers* were Mount Airey and Uncle Sam.

For real style, the *pigeonniers* at Houmas House on the River Road at Burnside are outstanding. Their lines have the appearance of being contemporary and they stand well and boldly next to their plantation house. There are reproductions, too; the one at Seven Oaks (Kenner) is the most perfect reproduction of a 1795 *pigeonnier* that one could expect to find. Made of old red brick with a cedar shingle roof, it makes an interesting garden feature.

If plantation and country gardens cornered a part of the market that was uniquely theirs, it was in their fine structures—the *pigeonnier*, the *garçonnière*, and their kin.

THIS SQUARE, RED BRICK PIGEONNIER HAS BEEN CONSTRUCTED IN THE STYLE OF A GENUINE EXAMPLE OF 1795. SET CLOSE TO THE HOUSE AND NEXT TO AN HERB GARDEN, IT IS CONNECTED BY A PERGOLA FESTOONED WITH WISTERIA AND LADY BANKSIA ROSES. (ANDRESSEN, SEVEN OAKS, KENNER)

4

Old Faithfuls

Heirloom Plants along the River Corridor

Among them—for I will mention a few—which represented

every clime, were the crape myrtle, with its pure

and delicately formed flower, the oak geranium,

the classical ivy, and the fragrant snow-drop. The broad

walks were, as usual in southern gardens, bordered

by the varnished lauria mundi, *occasionally relieved*

by the Cape jessamine, slender althea, and dark

green arborvitae. The splendidly attired amaryllis, the

purple magnolia, the Arabian and night-blooming

jessamines, the verbenum, or lemon-scented geranium . . .

JOSEPH HOLT INGRAHAM • 1835

he sheer joy of growing plants in the lower Mississippi valley is probably unsurpassed in any other region of the country. Even outside any context of design, the curiosity for growing and exhibiting plants for personal pleasure is a passion for many and a recreational hobby shared by the whole family for others. It involves all segments of the population and knows no social or economic bounds. There are plant lovers in every part of southern culture. This region surely has its share of gardening skeptics who moan and groan about conditions being too hot, too cold, too wet, or too dry. But the fact of the matter is that no other region of the country can boast of having so many optimum conditions coming together in a single area.

The Mississippi River corridor straddles two of the most prolific plant zones: zone 8 to the north favors a large selection of the more temperate species, while in zone 9 to the south many of the tropicals flourish. As far north as St. Francisville, Martha Turnbull noted in a November 1855 diary entry: "My orange trees are full of oranges," and on another occasion she mentioned planting artichokes in October. On the other hand, a freeze occurring on December 12, 1849 "killed all our roses."

Indeed, cold hardiness is probably the most limiting factor influencing plant distribution, although isolated microclimates

THIS DELIGHTFUL CRESCENT OF CHERUBS CAPTURES THE BRIGHT, ETHEREAL NATURE OF THE LOUISIANA WOODLANDS IN THE SPRING. THE FIGURES HAVE BEEN GIVEN A

RICH BACKDROP OF NATIVE SPECIES, INCLUDING HONEYSUCKLE AZALEA AND OTHER WOODLAND PLANTS. (AFTON VILLA, ST. FRANCISVILLE)

exist throughout the region; and within these special climate zones gardeners glean great pleasure in pushing to the limit the range of their favorite plants. Moisture is normally more than adequate for growing most plants, but the distribution of rainfall is unpredictable, thus requiring special water management practices at certain times of the year. The soil is relatively fertile and favors cultivation of a wide assortment of plants. With slight alterations to the soil, gardeners have an even larger number of planting options. And ameliorating soils by adding sand and humus to improve drainage and increase water-holding capacity can enhance flowering, fruiting, and other special seasonal features.

*T*he mainstay plants in southern gardens have changed relatively little over the past 150 years. Early flower and seed catalogs provide primary sources of information about what plants were being purchased and some trends in gardening practices. Art prints, garden plats and drawings, eighteenth- and nineteenth-century encyclopedias, almanacs, city property maps, old deeds, land transactions, personal diaries, and old medical

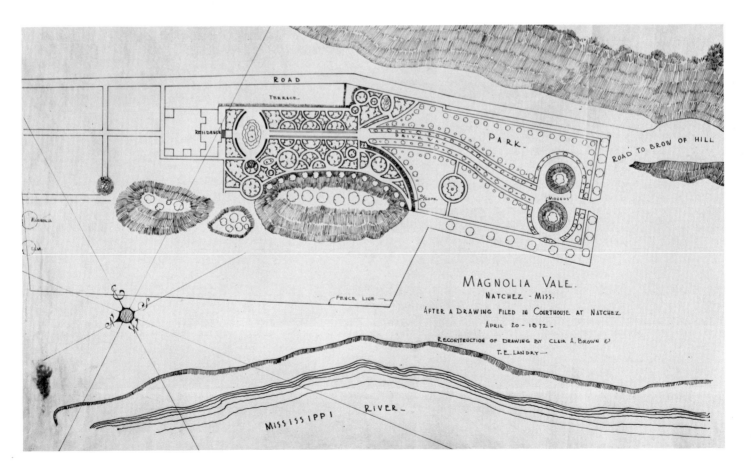

MAGNOLIA VALE, OR "BROWN'S GARDENS," AFTER A 1872 DRAWING FILED IN THE NATCHEZ COURTHOUSE, BY CLAIR A. BROWN AND T. E. LANDRY. AMONG NATCHEZ'S MOST RENOWNED MID-NINETEENTH-CENTURY GARDENS, MAGNOLIA VALE WAS FILLED WITH CLIPPED TOPIARIES, ROSES, AND OTHER HEIRLOOM PLANTS, AND WAS STRATEGICALLY SITED ON THE NATCHEZ BLUFFS CLOSE TO THE MISSISSIPPI RIVER WHERE STEAMERS STOPPED FOR GALA SOCIAL EVENTS. (THEODORE E. LANDRY COLLECTION, LOUISIANA STATE UNIVERSITY)

HONEYSUCKLE AZALEA.

Leaning over the picket fence, this old tea rose, cultivar 'Mrs. B. R. Cant,' recreates a scene familiar on many a plantation from 150 years ago. Tea roses were originally introduced from China. (Magnolia Mound)

The Cherokee rose (Rosa laevigata) is a rampant rambler that scrambles up hedgerows and trees, all over the woodlands. Used prudently in the garden, it makes a useful contribution to vertical gardening. (Highland Road, Baton Rouge)

GLOWING IN THE SHADE OF LIGHT TREE CANOPIES, THIS OLD VARIETY OF A SOUTHERN INDIAN AZALEA, (RHODODENDRON INDICUM) 'JOHN BULL,' IS RARE AND SELDOM SEEN. PRESERVED AT THE RURAL LIFE MUSEUM, THIS IS ONE OF THE LAST REMAINING STOCK OF ITS TYPE.

books provide glimpses into the interests of the day and give valuable information on the plants grown over the past two centuries. Much more extensive data is available on the horticulture of the region than on design. Today, accelerated hybridization and propagation practices are surely changing the picture in plant diversity and market availability for many of the herbaceous plants. With every passing season there are new offerings.

There is evidence that the typical nineteenth-century plantation homes were surrounded with a variety of ornamental plants, as well as plants prized for more utilitarian reasons. First, there were native species in fields and forests yielding an abundance of fruits and other useful items for daily plantation life. These included the wax myrtle, which supplied berries for making the all-important candles; various grasslike plants used for basket weaving; and the *barbe espagnole* (Spanish moss) that was used in mattress stuffings and in earlier days as a major ingredient in *bousillage*, a wall construction of moss, animal hair, and local mud. During hard times, the moss was also an important fiber food for cattle, and Martha Turnbull used moss as a mulch around her plants during periods of drought. The fruiting plants were valuable for their seasonal offerings for cooking and canning purposes—grapes, persimmons, plums, blackberries, pecans, and hawthorns, to name a few.

Central to all nineteenth-century plantation operations was the kitchen. Fortunately there are numerous accounts from old cooking instructions, or "receipts," that document the widespread dependence on a huge assortment of vegetable plants and culinary herbs. Diaries, bills of sales, catalogs, and newspaper and journal advertisements also shed considerable light on these essential groups of plants. Herbs required a relatively small parcel of land and were located close to the kitchen, while the row crops, the more space-consuming vegetables, were situated out in the larger fields.

Mammoth quantities of fresh foods were required to supply the needs of a typical plantation population of several hundred inhabitants. An advertisement in the *Baton Rouge Gazette* (October 29, 1831) provides examples of some of the most common and frequently referred to plants grown in the early kitchen gardens. It lists nine kinds of cabbages, six each of peas and beans, five of turnips and lettuces, and four kinds of beets and radishes. There are three kinds each of onions, squashes, and spinach, two each of mustard, carrots, and parsley, and the list also includes melons, "roquette," cayenne peppers, asparagus, leeks, chervil, cow cabbage, parsnips, and "mammoth" squash.

Also vital to self-contained plantation life were the medicinal herbs. Old medical books and journals provide fascinating insight into the range of plants reported to cure nearly every ailment known to humankind—a concoction of mustard and water was used to cure food poisoning, for example, while garlic

*AZALEAS WERE
INTRODUCED TO
THE PLANTATION
GARDENS IN THE
MID-NINETEENTH
CENTURY.
(ROSEDOWN)*

was taken to reduce fever, and a compound of camphor and other ingredients was the prescription to control rheumatism. And there was the all-important herb, costmary, sometimes referred to as "Bible leaf" (*Chrysanthemum Balsamita*), because it was frequently used as a Bible bookmark, and it was called upon at times for its invigorating scent to keep churchgoers awake during long sermons.

Valcour Aime, reported to be one of the South's wealthiest plantation owners, imported the exotic fruits and other useful plants to his home, Petite Versailles (1799), in St. James Parish about fifty miles north of New Orleans. Plants once grown at this now ruined garden included bananas, pineapples, mangoes, Perique tobacco, and coffee. Unfortunately, little is left today on the site of this plantation. The ruins hold the secrets of how gardening was practiced in the grand style on one very influential river plantation during the early nineteenth century.

*P*rosperous times associated with the mid-nineteenth-century South brought a new and exotic group of plants to the forefront: those today known as ornamentals or decorative plants. Prior to this time there was likely little interest in or time

MOUNDS OF SPIREAS WERE TYPICAL AROUND PLANTATION HOMES. EQUALLY POPULAR IN CONTEMPORARY GARDENS, THE ARCHING STEMS OF THE REEVES SPIREA (SPIRAEA CANTONIENSIS) ARE LADEN WITH FLOWERS FOR SEVERAL WEEKS IN EARLY SPRING. (TEZCUCO PLANTATION, BURNSIDE)

for working with plants for purely esthetic purposes except by the relatively small number of truly affluent landowners and city dwellers. But increasingly, the uncultivated wilderness was deemed insufficient, despite its wild beauty, and the huge farmlands were themselves intimidating. More and more, human handiwork was imposed upon the land—spaces were carved out of the rustic landscapes and gardens were formed, crude though they might have been compared to those in the ancestral countries.

By 1840 there was already a New World instruction manual in the form of T. Bridgeman's *The Young Gardener's Assistant*, offering sound counsel:

> One important point to be attended to is to have a
> supply of good old manure, and other composts ready to
> incorporate with the earth; also a portion of ashes, soot,

MASSED HYDRANGEAS MAKE A BOLD STATEMENT UNDER THE TREES AT ROSEDOWN.

THE DOUBLE WHITE FLOWERS OF THE FLOWERING CHERRY.

tobacco dust, and lime for the purpose of sowing over seed beds in the dry weather.

To this end, he may form a border round the whole garden, from five to ten feet wide according to the size of the piece of land; next to this border, a walk may be made from three to six feet wide; the centre part of the garden may be divided into squares on the sides of which a border may be laid out three to four feet wide.

*E*arly European gardens contained a relatively limited number of plant species, actually fewer than the number native in the New World. It was not until trade routes were opened and exploratory trips into Asia grew more frequent that there was a big influx of new plants into western gardens. The period between 1750 and 1850, sometimes called the "golden age"

MANY VARIETIES OF CAMELLIAS WERE CULTIVATED IN ENGLAND AND WESTERN EUROPE DURING THE EIGHTEENTH CENTURY. SEVERAL OF THESE MADE THEIR WAY TO AMERICA. THIS VARIETY OF JAPANESE CAMELLIA, 'PAULETTE GODDARD,' WAS POPULAR EARLIER THIS CENTURY AND STILL HOLDS SWAY AS AN OUTSTANDING PERFORMER, BLOOMING IN SPRING WELL AFTER MOST OTHER CAMELLIAS. HOUMAS HOUSE.

THE OLD VARIETIES OF THE CANNA HAD MUCH SMALLER FLOWERS BORNE ON LONGER STEMS THAN PRESENT-DAY HYBRIDS. THIS VARIETY OF CANNA × GENERALIS FINDS ITS ORIGINAL POSITION AT THE FOOT OF A LARGE PILLAR AT OAK ALLEY, VACHERIE.

LIKE MANY OF THE OLD FAVORITES OF THE PLANTATION GARDENS, THE JAPANESE ROSE (KERRIA JAPONICA) PROVIDES BRIGHT COLOR AMONG THE OTHER SPRING FLOWERS. IT WAS INTRODUCED FROM THE EAST IN THE EIGHTEENTH CENTURY. (ROSALIE, NATCHEZ)

of plant introduction, was the most important period for starting new plants in the United States. Tens of thousands of plants were brought into the country from all parts of the world. The great gardens of England and Europe had sent out collectors to China, Japan, and other countries. Plant explorers were adventuresome people who would go to any extreme to locate new plants for experimentation. It is reported that E.H. Wilson shipped over 1,000 new species to the Arnold Arboretum in Boston from his explorations to China, while Charles S. Sargent, another American plant explorer, was equally zealous in his search for plants in Japan.

In the United States, prestigious plant societies like the Pennsylvania Horticultural Society, founded in 1827, and the Massachusetts Horticultural Society, formed in 1829, were equally ambitious in their quest for new plant introductions. During the same period some fine American plants like phlox, coreopsis, gaillardia, and other annuals were transported to European gardens, only to return as improved hybrid forms. The giant Mexican marigold, for example, which was reported to have been fed to chickens to make the egg yolks a dark color, was sent to

France, and returned some years later in improved hybrid forms. By the mid-nineteenth century, a considerable trade in exotic ornamentals was taking place.

While there was an abundance of indigenous plants to use as gardening material in the South, most of them blended with the natural fabric of the native landscape, and gardeners were increasingly eager to set aside parcels of land distinct from the woodland where their new plants acquired from friends or mail-order houses could be exhibited. The prolific diarist Martha Turnbull of Rosedown underscores the point—note that these entries span fifty years: "Received things from Cincinnati," she wrote on November 15, 1841; "9 more roses from Louisville" in January 1891, and "sent to Thompson & Sons for Roses and Dahlias," in November 1892.

From China came all-time favorites like roses, bridal wreath spirea, crape myrtle, Chinese varnish, gardenia, and tea olive—the latter having traditionally been used for perfuming tea. From Japan came many notables which had the species name "japonica." Popular imports from Japan included camellia, azalea, flowering almond, cryptomeria, and boxwood (*Buxus macrophylla*). The very first box introduced to the South was *Buxus sempervirens* 'Suffructicosa,' an early import originally from England. This selection grows quite large and irregular and tends to be affected by several soil-borne pests. Many southern gardeners have greater successes with *macrophylla* with its more

COCKSCOMB (CELOSIA CRISTATA), WHICH COMES IN SEVERAL BRILLIANT COLORS, WAS AN OLD FAVORITE AROUND FARM BUILDINGS AND PROVIDED USEFUL SPLASHES OF COLOR IN THE FALL. IT WAS ALSO USED IN THE PAST FOR FLORAL ARRANGEMENTS IN FALL AND WINTER. (ST. FRANCISVILLE)

BOTH SPANISH MOSS AND BALD CYPRESS ARE NATIVES TO THE MISSISSIPPI RIVER CORRIDOR. NOW PLANTED WIDELY, THE CYPRESS IS STILL A HAVEN FOR SPANISH MOSS. AS WILLIAM BARTRAM SAID IN THE 1770S: "THE BALD CYPRESS STANDS IN THE FIRST ORDER OF NORTH AMERICAN TREES. ITS MAJESTIC STATURE IS SURPRISING; AND ON APPROACHING IT, WE ARE STRUCK WITH A KIND OF AWE AT BEHOLDING THE STATELINESS OF THE TRUNK LIFTING ITS CUMBROUS TOP TOWARDS THE SKIES . . ."(CRUIKSHANK). (CITY PARK, NEW ORLEANS)

delightful green glow when the new leaves thrust forward in spring. Forsthyia also came from the Orient to decorate the grounds of plantation homes in the upper part of the region.

Early roses from France and Spain, finding their way to the United States via England, adorned many a garden and yard. In contemporary gardens throughout the region, these old roses, sometimes referred to as "antique" roses, are finding new favor. Their revival is due in part to the research work and promotion conducted by Dr. William C. Welch of Texas A&M University and the Southern Garden History Society. Welch's books, *Perennial Garden Color* and *Antique Roses for the South*, provide interesting insights into early plantings as well as renewed enthusiasm for these plants as creative expressions in today's gardens. Special organizations like the Southern Garden History Society and the Southern Garden Symposium (St. Francisville) have among their primary objectives research about and promotion of old garden plants and garden preservation.

*W*ith the favorable growing conditions of the region, populations of the introduced species exploded because most plants could easily be propagated by divisions, cuttings, and, for some species, by seeds. At the same time, greenhouses, cold frames, and other horticulture structures were springing up as necessary components to the landscape—first for providing early seedlings for the vegetables, but increasingly having some space allocated for propagation of favorite ornamentals. Plant sharing has always been a strong tradition in southern culture, and swapping with neighbors and friends resulted in a rapid distribution of successful new arrivals. Precious few of the truly showy garden plants were native in origin to the region. The natives that were grown as ornamentals had great difficulty competing with the drama of exotic imports.

FLOWERING IN THE BAYOUS, SWAMPS, AND OTHER WETLANDS ALONG THE MISSISSIPPI RIVER WERE A COLLECTION OF FIVE NATIVE SPECIES OF LOUISIANA IRIS IN BLUE, RED, YELLOW, WHITE, AND PURPLE COLORS. THESE ORIGINAL IRISES ARE IMPORTANT HORTICULTURALLY BECAUSE CROSSES HAVE RESULTED IN MANY EXQUISITE MODERN HYBRIDS. (MAGNOLIA MOUND)

Listed here are some of the Mississippi River corridor garden favorites from the nineteenth century and the early part of the twentieth, along with the approximate dates that the plants were introduced to the United States. Information was derived from several sources, primarily from unpublished papers in the Theodore E. Landry collection in the Hill Memorial Library, Louisiana State University, Baton Rouge. Mr. and Mrs. Landry traveled throughout the country presenting lectures on plantings in eighteenth- and nineteenth-century gardens. Their lecture notes reference *Gardens and Gardeners of the American Colonies, and of The Republic Before 1840* by Alice B. Lockwood, and *Origins of American Horticulture*, a handbook published by the Brooklyn Botanical Gardens.

PLANTS INTRODUCED TO U.S. GARDENS

HERBACEOUS PLANTS BEFORE 1700

ANEMONES	HOUSE LEEK
CARNATION, OR	MARTAGON LILIES
CLOVE PINK	NARCISSUS
(DIANTHUS)	PRIMROSE
COLUMBINE	SATIN FLOWER
CROWN IMPERIAL	SCARLET CROSS
DOUBLE MARIGOLD	STAR OF BETHLEHEM
(CALENDULA)	SUNFLOWER
GRAPE FLOWER,	
OR MUSCARI	
HEMEROCALLIS	
HOLLYHOCK	

1700–1750

AMARANTHUS	JACOB'S LADDER
BACHELOR BUTTON	LILAC
BELL FLOWER	LILY OF THE VALLEY
CANDYTUFT	PEONY
DEVIL IN A BUSH	PERIWINKLE
FRAXINELLA	SOUTHERNWOOD
	SPIDERWORT

1750–1800

ALOES	MAGNOLIAS
CLETHRA	MORNING GLORY
DOUBLE CHINA PINKS	*NARCISSI POETICUS*
DOUBLE LARKSPUR	*FLORA PLENA*
ENGLISH IVY	OLEANDER
HONEYSUCKLE	ORANGES
GLADIOLUS	PASSIONFLOWER
(COMMON FLAG)	PERSIAN IRIS
LIMES	SNAPDRAGON

THE WHITE FORM OF THE FLOWERING DOGWOOD (CORNUS FLORIDA) IS THE MOST COMMON IN GARDENS. THE GREATLY ADMIRED FLOWERING TREE IS ABUNDANT WHERE SOILS ARE SANDY AND WELL DRAINED AND WHERE THERE IS LIGHT SHADE FOR MOST OF THE DAY. THERE ARE SEVERAL CULTIVARS WITH PINK FLOWERS, ACTUALLY "BRACTS," OR MODIFIED LEAVES.

OTHER PLANTS IN EARLY GARDENS
ALONG THE MISSISSIPPI RIVER

AGAVE, OR
CENTURY PLANT
ALTHAEA, OR
ROSE OF
SHARON
ARBORVITAE
BRIDAL WREATH
BOX
CAMELLIA
CHINABERRY,
CHICKEN TREE,
"PRIDE OF INDIA"*
CHINESE WISTERIA
CRAPE MYRTLE
DEUTZIA
FLOWERING
ALMOND
FLOWERING
QUINCE

FORSYTHIA, OR
GOLDEN-BELLS
GARDENIA, OR
CAPE JASMINE
IVY
MOCK ORANGE
MAGNOLIA FUSCATA,
OR BANANA SHRUB
OLEANDER
SWEET OLIVE, OR
FRAGRANT
OLIVE
SWEET SHRUB,
CAROLINA
ALLSPICE,
STRAWBERRY
SHRUB
YUCCA

*NOTE: "Pride of India" has also been used as a name for
crape myrtle, Lagerstroemia speciosa, and the golden rain
tree, Koelreuteria paniculata, according to Hortus Third.

A description of some of the plants that were actually in
plantation gardens can be read in Joseph Holt Ingraham's record of
his excursions in the area in 1835. His epigraph opening this
chapter is about a fine garden he visited on a "two hours ride" from
Natchez, "said to be the finest garden in Mississippi," and to that
list of more than a dozen old favorites he adds:

> ...with the majestic aloe [not an Aloe as we know it
> today, but an Agave], that hoary monarch of the garden,
> which blooms but once in a century, the broad-leaved
> yarra, or caco [Yucca], the fragrant snow-drop, and the
> sweet-scented shrub and oleander, with countless other
> shrubs and flowers, breathing forth the sweetest fra-
> grance, gratified the senses, and pleased the eye wher-
> ever it was turned. There spread the cassia [Indigo], a
> creeping plant, bearing a pink flower...

Other early travelers to the region were also impressed: "I
entered the front yard—a green level, shaded with the relics

A RIOT OF SPRING PHLOX UNDERSCORES THE
RUINS OF AFTON VILLA, WHERE ONCE A FINE
GOTHIC MANSION STOOD. THE SPRING
PHLOX, A HARDY PERENNIAL, BLOOMS FOR
NEARLY TWO MONTHS, BEGINNING IN LATE
FEBRUARY.

A MUCH MORE PETITE VARIETY OF THE
MAGNOLIA IS 'LITTLE GEM,' WHICH GROWS
TO ABOUT FIFTEEN FEET. IT HAS LARGE
FLOWERS AND RICH BROWN UNDERSIDES TO
ITS LEAVES. (ALMA PLANTATION, LAKELAND)

NATIVE AND INTRODUCED PLANTINGS, SUCH
AS SPIREA AND DAFFODILS, GIVE THIS LIGHT
WOODLAND THE NATURALISTIC AMBIENCE
THAT IS SIMILAR TO WOODLANDS IN
SOUTHEAST ENGLAND. AFTON VILLA.

of a forest—the live oak, sycamore, and gum trees"; of a scene in Natchez: "A beautiful avenue bordered with the luxuriant China tree, the 'Pride of China,' whose dark rich foliage, nearly meeting above, formed a continued arcade as far as the eye could penetrate. . . . The China tree yields in beauty to no other. This, as I have before remarked, is the universal shade tree for cabin and villa in this state."

As Ingraham and others recorded, among the traditional plants grown in plantation gardens and especially near the house were the highly scented flowering plants. These included the sweet olive, banana shrub, sweet shrub, mock orange, magnolia, and jessamine, to name a few. Their powerful, evocative fragrances would pervade the gallery and open interiors. They would herald in the spring and perfume the March air. The sweet olive and banana shrub—both long-lived, dominant, large evergreen shrubs— would serve as major "anchor" plants in prominent positions in the landscape near the front door or at the corners of houses.

Legend holds that one group of especially aromatic plants were sometimes referred to as the "bosom" plants. There were several. The sweet olive with its highly scented tiny white flowers, the banana shrub with its banana-scented, magnolia-shaped flowers, and the burgundy-colored flowers of the Carolina sweet shrub, which have a ripened apple or pineapplelike fragrance, were often favored with a spot beside the front door or front steps of the mansion. Here they were handy plants from which a sprig could be cut and placed in a fair lady's bosom as she departed for a special occasion.

In Europe, scented plants had been long used in tightly arranged masses called nosegays, carried by ladies close to the nose so that only pleasant smells were savored even in evil-smelling places. In her *Social Life in Old New Orleans*, Eliza Ripley reminisces about nosegays, which were prevalent there when she was a girl in the 1840s. On some portions of a southern plantation, where there were many animals or fermenting sugar cane and cattle feed, ladies would no doubt also have welcomed nosegays to stifle the odorous wafts of farming operations.

As was indicated for antique roses, many of the other old flowering species mentioned here lost favor for a time because they became viewed as commonplace; but they are now being reclaimed in garden restoration activities. They are being selected for contemporary gardens because of their attractive features in addition to their ability to survive and perform well without a lot of attention and maintenance by contrast to some of the newer introduced species.

CEMETERIES ARE A LIVING GENE BANK OF HEIRLOOM PLANT MATERIAL, SOME OF WHICH HAVE WEATHERED THE VAGARIES OF THE WIND, RAIN, AND SEARING HEAT FOR MORE THAN 150 YEARS UNTENDED BY MAN. OLD FAVORITES FLOURISH AND ARE PROPAGATED IN THE INTEREST OF BOTANICAL HISTORY, AS HERE WITH THE OLD EVERGREEN AZALEA 'CHRISTMAS CHEER' AT THE CEMETERY OF GRACE CHURCH IN ST. FRANCISVILLE.

GARDENIAS (GARDENIA JASMINOIDES) HAVE THEIR ORIGINS IN CHINA. (GREG GRANT)

THE MAGNOLIA (MAGNOLIA GRANDIFLORA) IS THE STATE FLOWER FOR BOTH LOUISIANA AND MISSISSIPPI. A NATIVE OF THE SOUTHERN STATES, THE LARGE TREE WITH COARSE-TEXTURED LEAVES MAKES A BOLD STATEMENT IN THE STRUCTURE OF GARDENS. THE SHOWY, HANDSOME FLOWERS LAST ONLY A DAY AND ATTRACT LOTS OF HONEYBEES WITH ITS STRONG SCENT, WHICH PERVADES THE STILL, HUMID AIR OF SOUTHERN GARDENS.

Although in the early days natives came to be considered less worthy than imports, such plants nevertheless had their place as reliable performers. Considerable attention is now being given to the natives by special organizations like the Native Plant Society at its national conferences and regional symposia. Indeed, the United States has been a major contributor of plants to other countries. Some of the favorites in gardens abroad had their beginnings in the wilds of North America, These include several of the magnolias, bald cypress, maples, oaks, dogwood, and sumac, among the many trees and shrubs. Herbaceous species in this category include goldenrod, blazing star, blue lobelia, hibiscus, spiderwort, bergamot (*Monarda*), and Virginia creeper. Some of these, like bergamot, figure strongly in typical Jekyllian color borders both in the South and overseas.

5

Water in the Garden

Into "La Riviere" the water

was drawn by pumps from the river,

slipping through the mouths

of brass swans set on a wall.

NINETEENTH-CENTURY ACCOUNT
QUOTED IN *PLANTATION PARADE* • 1945

oothing, tranquil, captivating, dazzling, stimulating, magical, exciting, reflective, playful, and musical are but a few of the adjectives that describe the value and moods of water in garden design. Ancient paintings and other records of humanity's first relationship with nature in a garden setting clearly indicate that water was the first of many elements to be introduced. As a life-sustaining force in the harsh, dry landscapes where western civilizations began, water was an essential commodity. The early Persian, Moorish, and Italian gardens would have been lifeless without the sound of water. The echo of water was obligatory, just as the appreciation of its reflective qualities from a belevedere later became.

The position of water in ancient gardens exceeded that of flower color in importance. It helped to emphasize variations in grade by puncuating each level change with sound, and providing special cooling effects as it moved downhill.

The role of water in both early and contemporary gardens along the Mississippi is as crucial as its place in gardens around the world. It is the substance that gives the entire region its special ambience for producing and sustaining a lush, near-tropical environment, as well as being among the most sought-after elements in garden enrichment.

SPLASHING WATER PLAYS MYSTERIOUSLY ON THE WATERS OF THE WOODLAND POOL. (AFTON VILLA, ST. FRANCISVILLE)

Water is one of those special materials that can be appreciated without understanding all of its mysterious qualities. It has the power to change a garden's atmosphere and character more dramatically than anything else. A quiet, dismal place can be brought alive with moving water. Its lively qualities have been used in a thousand different ways to set scenes and moods, from elegant garden spaces with formal fountains, or sheets of serenely passive, reflective surfaces, to light, airy sprays that sparkle cheerfully in bright sunlight. Channeled and guided over and around rock, or across surfaces of many materials, it can be "tuned" to emulate the effects of a woodland stream fed by a natural spring.

*I*n short, no garden element has the power to "draw" people into the presence of a space quite like water. As a focal point it has no equal. Contemporary designers continue to study and use its mysterious qualities, as have gardeners through the centuries.

Water is surely no stranger to people who have lived for generations along the Mississippi River. Plantation gardens grew up beside the mighty Mississippi and were in a sense entirely

A TIMELESS SCENE AS SPANISH MOSS ALMOST TOUCHES THE WATER HYACINTH AND WATER LETTUCE IN THE SUGAR KETTLE BELOW IT AT PARLANGE PLANTATION, NEW ROADS. AS BARTRAM REMARKED, "THE LONG MOSS, SO CALLED, (TILLANDSIA USNEOIDES), IS A SINGULAR AND SURPRISING VEGETABLE PRODUCTION."

THE FOCAL POINT AT THE END OF A LONG AXIS THAT PASSES THROUGH THE GARDEN, THIS FOUNTAIN MAKES MUSIC AT THE DIVIDING OF THE WAYS. (ROSEDOWN)

dominated by it. Design of gardens was nearly always strongly influenced by the presence of the river, usually at the far end of the *allée* from the plantation house.

The design of the elevated houses reflected the frequent demands the river would have on the flat land bordering its marshy margins. Many an early plantation garden would have been wrecked by seasonal flooding had it not been for the natural deposits of soil directly adjacent to the river. Natural levees were formed close to the river's main channel and occasionally these levees were not adequate to withstand the ravages of the mighty Mississippi's power.

A more dramatic link with the river is seen in Natchez, which is perched high on bluffs several hundred feet above the Mississippi. Few places in the world have such a striking setting, where a dynamic body of water is incorporated into the landscape to as profound a degree as one experiences at Rosalie, Magnolia Vale, and the Briars on the Natchez bluffs. In the cases of Rosalie in Natchez and Houmas House downriver, the belvederes set in the roofs served utilitarian as well as esthetic purposes: a belvedere was a look-out point to determine when master mariners and heads of houses were on their way back home.

THE CENTERPIECE OF THIS YELLOW-GREEN GARDEN IS THE SUGAR KETTLE. THE GARDEN COLORS COMPLEMENT THE COLORS OF THE NINETEENTH-CENTURY HOUSE, WHICH WAS SHIPPED PREFABRICATED BY BARGE FROM OHIO TO NATCHEZ ON THE MISSISSIPPI RIVER. (BARNES, NATCHEZ)

Not only were plantation gardens thus dominated by views of the turbulent waters from the precarious lowlands or from the safety of the Natchez hills, but water was often incorporated into the garden design itself. Water playing and babbling was a gentle reminder of far-off places—perhaps of summer tours of European gardens. The design reflected this strong European influence especially where stone figures, water music, and different levels in the garden united. Water can be choreographed to provide pleasant surprises for unsuspecting visitors who turn corners and encounter these special delights, where water provides the setting for distinctive shifts in tone. Water can be active and playful when carefully controlled by pressure and regulated nozzles; or it can be still and reflective in a formal, elegant setting.

*T*he sound of water adds tremendous value to any garden experience, and is especially refreshing in the sultry southern heat. Tumbling and tinkling water guided over stones, other textured surfaces, or over weirs is magical, giving gardens an extra

PLAYING TWO PIPES AT THE SAME TIME, THIS MUSICIAN WELCOMES VISITORS TO PARLANGE PLANTATION NEAR NEW ROADS.

A WALL OF CASCADING WATER REFRESHES THE AIR IN THIS TINY COURTYARD GARDEN IN BATON ROUGE. LOTUS PLANTS ARE AT THE FOOT OF THE CASCADE. LEGEND HOLDS THAT BUDDAH WAS BORN IN THE LARGE PINK BLOOM OF THE LOTUS. (EMERSON AND ASSOCIATES, BATON ROUGE)

quality of enjoyment, a special sense of place, and sometimes making a visit a never-to-be-forgotten experience. Concealed from immediate sight, the sounds of water can beckon the least inquisitive person to its source—a theme often beautifully executed in the Oriental garden tradition. The ethos of water is taken a lot more seriously in Japan than in most of the United States. In a *karasansui* garden setting, the garden materials are actually wetted before important visitors arrive, since wet stones and foliage yield impressive visual properties barely suspected when they are dry.

The effect of light on water can be riveting, as Monet appreciated in his water lily pond. Passing clouds, intermingled with the tantalizing shadows and reflections of overhanging trees and shrubs, cast intriguing images over the water. Natural sunlight, the angle of the sun, the time of day or night, and artificial illumination are among the forces that can affect garden design with water dramatically.

For example, still water under live oaks is black and moody, but still water under a clear blue sky is light and more transparent. The white and blue through which a garden is perceived as a reflection in the water can be airy and revealing since the ultraviolet is taken out of the light, leaving a picture clearer than that which the eye perceives in reality. As Peter Coates, in *Great Gardens*, described the effect of water at Versailles, there were "pieces of water laid to lighten the cold perfection of the perspec-

A GARDEN POND IS A FEATURED ELEMENT OF THE GARDEN OF NOTTOWAY PLANTATION, LOUISIANA'S LARGEST PLANTATION HOME.

A NATURALISTIC GARDEN AND POOL AT LONGUE VUE GARDENS.

tive with their glimpses of the sky, where we are almost surprised to see the still undistorted clouds sail by."

One garden along the Mississippi which stands alone for its indulgence in the pleasures of water is Longue Vue Gardens in New Orleans. Water was incorporated into the early work by landscape architect Ellen Shipman in 1935. Later alterations indicate a strong Moorish influence. The renowned landscape architect Wiiliam Platt and the owners visited the Generalife gardens of Granada in southern Spain specifically to absorb these Moorish/Spanish ideas. The final interpretation at Longue Vue is Moorish fourteenth-century with American concessions. But there are English, Italian, and Grecian connections too.

Longue Vue combines many garden designs associated with water, from traditional pools, fountains and a *jet d'eau* to a range of contemporary water sculptures. There is one sugar kettle surreptitiously sunken into the ground as the centerpiece of the Walled Garden where its design features are attractively employed.

The Longue Vue mansion was built in Greek Revival style in the late 1940s around an existing garden. In fact, the eight acres of grounds modeled after an English country seat have two inherent styles based on water, the Spanish Court Garden and the Portugese Canal Garden.

THE SIGHT AND
SOUND OF WATER
IN THE GARDEN
ARE PERFECTLY
CELEBRATED AT
LONGUE VUE,
WHOSE WATER
GARDENS WERE
INSPIRED BY
THOSE AT THE
GENERALIFE IN
GRANADA, SPAIN.

Incredibly, there are twenty-three fountain displays at Longue Vue, most of them small and influenced by those at Generalife. The most impressive of all is the Spanish Garden fountain, a long pool aligned with the grand *allée* from the house, into which play ten pairs of arching water jets. At Longue Vue the fountains are set in their own small spaces of brick and pebble.

The large Three Graces fountain in the forecourt of the mansion is Victorian and depicts the classical theme of the three graces—Aglaia, Thalia, and Euphrosyne—said to have presided over the elegant arts. The piece is probably American, but there are no markings to link it with a specific foundry. Kenneth Lynch Foundry of Wilton, Connecticut cast many of the water pieces. A contemporary piece is a water mobile sculpture in the Spanish Court Garden. A scene of tumbling dolphins that move as the water plays on them, it is entitled "Arabesque" and is made of white bronze. The design is by famous New Orleans sculptor, Lin Emery. A statue of Pan was sculpted by the British sculptress, Josephine Knoblock, and the contemporary bronze fountain in the Yellow Garden is the work of Robert Engman, a Philadelphia sculptor.

Many other New Orleans gardens utilize water in highly creative ways. The small, intimate spaces of private courtyards and other settings offer excellent opportunities to use water imaginatively in fountains and pools incorporated into walls of the outdoor spaces.

In early days, the people of New Orleans lived perpetually with the threat of inundation. Living at or even below sea level and at times beneath the high-water level of the mighty Mississippi, everyone had a healthy respect for the power of water. Because of a high water table, gardening in early times presented special horticulture problems, as it still does today. At certain times of the year, when a hole is dug in the existing terrain, it immediately fills with unwanted water. Consequently, plantings are by necessity elevated to compensate for the high groundwater level. Survival of trees, shrubs, and even certain herbaceous plants set into waterlogged soils is assured by elevating beds well above existing soils. With most of their roots above the soaked soils, plants tend to fare better.

*P*lantations along the river corridor often had lakes or small ponds which added to the ambience of the overall landscape settings. The garden pond at the newly designed gardens at Monmouth in Natchez has utilized water in a most attractive fashion. Seen at a considerable distance from the upper terraces of the mansion, the plantings, garden bridge, and other structural elements on or adjacent to the pond have greatly enhanced this site by providing delightful details in what was once a more parklike setting.

At Hemingbough, near St. Francisville, water becomes the background for the entire development and, in many cases, the

AN INNER SANCTUM OF A SECRET GARDEN IN NEW ORLEANS PROVIDES A SIMPLE INTERLUDE FOR THOUGHT AND MEDITATION. SKIRTED BY RUSHES, WATER HYACINTH, AND LILIES, THE COMPOSITION IS RICH IN PLANTING DETAILS. (FRIERSON, NEW ORLEANS)

REFLECTED ACROSS A POND FULL OF FISH AND TURTLES, THE NEW BRIDGE LINKS SEVERAL IMPORTANT PARTS OF THE NEW DEVELOPMENT AT THE HISTORIC HOUSE AND GARDENS OF MONMOUTH IN NATCHEZ.

focus for special structures and use areas. The temple and its semicircular colonnade amphitheater is a structure similar to the one at Sibyl at Tivoli in Italy—a bold terrace perched above the water's edge with handsome garden embellishments. These are but a few of the striking features used in combination with water at Hemingbough. Other examples of eighteenth-century European and English influences are being incorporated into the plantation landscape developments throughout the region.

Sugar kettles, installations from the days when these were an integral aspect of the sugar cane industry, are common landmarks in many plantation gardens today. They are highly prized possessions and are seeing active service as garden accessories in many different ways in landscape restorations and even in the contemporary gardens.

SERENELY SETTLED IN A SUGAR KETTLE IN A LEAFY ENCLAVE OF THE WOODS, THIS EASTERN GENTLEMAN HAS PLENTY OF TIME TO CONTEMPLATE HIS BEAUTIFUL SURROUNDINGS. (BURDEN GARDEN, RURAL LIFE MUSEUM)

All along the river corridor, these old reminders of plantation life can be seen as isolated features on the open lawn, and many are the dominant water feature or planter under the broad, low-hanging limbs of an ancient live oak. Other sugar kettles are incorporated into the highly detailed and structured design of terraces, patios, and other outdoor spaces of old garden settings as well as new gardens of the urban areas. Because of their size—depth as well as width—they function satisfactorily as dry planters or as water features incorporating both plants and fish.

*A*lthough normally used as an element bringing great pleasure to the garden setting, water is sometimes used incorrectly. Water can easily overpower a space. As with all components of a landscape, overuse or improper use can make a garden feel crowded and uninviting. Overdesign in the amount and power of water under pressure can generate such harsh sounds that some spaces can become intimidating and may even repel people who might otherwise have found great delight in sitting for contemplation or conversation without the sound competition. When correctly conceived, designed, and installed, however, the sound of water can counteract outside noises and thus make gardens even more appealing, especially in cities.

Water plants play an important role in the gardens along the river. Introduced to provide special seasonal color and textural contrasts, they are sometimes planted directly in the pools, while for other water features they are maintained as container-grown specimens. The region enjoys a long growing season and mild winters; consequently foliage development and flower production are rapid. Under favorable growing conditions flowering plants can be expected to bloom profusely from mid-May until the first hard frost.

Several different types of plants are used with water depending on water depth, water quality, surface area, and,

IN A PRIVATE NEW ORLEANS GARDEN, THE
WATER POOL'S NATURALISTIC ARRANGEMENT
OF PLANTS INCLUDES WATER LILIES, PITCHER
PLANTS (IN A SPECIAL BOG COMPARTMENT),
FERNS, CYPERUS, AND AMERICAN CRINUMS.
(FREIBERG, NEW ORLEANS)

AN EXAMPLE OF VERTICAL AND HORIZONTAL
GARDENING IS SHOWN IN THIS ENCLOSED
COURTYARD GARDEN IN BATON ROUGE. LUSH
TROPICAL PLANTS HAVE BEEN CAREFULLY
GROUPED TO BEST UTILIZE THE SMALL SPACE.
(MORGAN, BATON ROUGE)

naturally, one's preference. The oxygenating or submerged species include such plants as water milfoil (*Myriophyllum*), elodea, water hawthorn (*Aponogeton*), and water-shield (*Cabomba*). Plants from this group are especially important for providing oxygen to the pools which contain fish.

For color, there are many included in the southern garden. The tropical and hardy water lilies include nearly every hue, with plant spread ranging from one to twelve feet. They grow in full sunlight to partial shade and there are both day and night bloomers. In large pools the exotic pond lotuses provide spectacular features. Other examples common to these gardens include the irises (*Siberian, Louisiana, crested, and Kaempferi*), water canna (*Canna*), red-stemmed canna (*Thalia*), water poppy (*Hydrocleys*), spider lily (*Hymenocallis*), pickerel weed (*Pontederia*), golden club (*orontium*), and bog lily (*Crinum*).

Exotic foliages providing great variations in textures are especially well adapted to this semi-tropical region. Among the most popular are dwarf and common umbrella plant (*Cyperus*), taro (*Colocasia*), spike rush (*Eleocharis*), sweet flag (*Acorus*), parrot's feather (*Myriophyllum*), and horsetail (*Equisetum*).

And there are endless choices of plants suitable as tubbed specimens that provide color throughout the seasons. Because of the mild climate, there is virtually no time when flowering plants cannot be used to further embellish the great diversity of water features in gardens along the Mississippi.

Keeping the Cold at Bay

Some are of [the] opinion that greenhouses are of no further

service than merely to store away a miscellaneous assortment of

rubbish during the months of winter, for the obvious purpose

of preserving them until the next summer ... What is or ought

to be, the chief ornament of the garden, [is] deprived of its

character, for want of taste, and divested of its interest, for

lack of skill. Visitors say, "Let us have a look at the green-

house." "No," replies the gardener apologetically, "it's not

worth your while going in, for there is nothing there to see."

A humiliating acknowledgement, but full of truth.

ROBERT LEUCHARS • 1854

otted around the gardens of the plantation homes along the Mississippi River, are several types of utility buildings intended to protect plants in cold weather. Hothouses, cold frames, greenhouses, and other horticulture structures became significant elements in some early gardens. They were not all merely utilitarian, however. Louisiana and Mississippi gardens have fine examples of these structures used as horticulture embellishments, and the location of such buildings indicates their importance to plantation operations.

It is said that an Englishman's house is his castle. To some keen gardeners, their potting shed or their greenhouse is indeed their pride and joy, even their castle. At Dunleith, in Natchez, such joys are encapsulated in a genuine English greenhouse sporting a stove room finished off with turrets, just like a small castle.

It must be said that in England—the founding country for many greenhouse designs—the mere presence of an old greenhouse or hothouse is not in itself noteworthy, and many are rather undistinguished. Since they are so common, unless they have unique features or are of a particularly unusual design, they often go unremarked, as most estates had one or more of these struc-

THIS CASTELLATED GREENHOUSE AT DUNLEITH IN NATCHEZ REFLECTS THE WEALTH AND OPULENCE OF THE VICTORIAN AGE. THE DESIGN IS VERY ENGLISH, THE MAGNIFICENCE VERY FRENCH.

SITTING MODESTLY BEHIND THE PICKET FENCE, THIS TIRED-LOOKING HOTHOUSE WAS ONCE THE PROPAGATING BACKBONE OF THE PLANTATION. (THE COTTAGE PLANTATION, ST. FRANCISVILLE)

tures. Along the Mississippi, however, these embellishments of English design influence stand out, simply because they are less common in these outposts of Old World influence. The involved process of getting the raw materials directly from England, or of lovingly copying English design, have made the Louisiana and Mississippi structures much more important, especially when they are restored to near perfection. Prefabricated sectional buildings were floated hundreds of miles down the Mississippi for construction in Natchez in the mid-nineteenth century, but getting a genuine greenhouse kit from Europe offered a challenge of a little more logistical planning.

*I*t was very much *de riguer* to be seen growing early seedlings for the vegetable gardens, as well as growing exciting and colorful tropicals. And plantation gardeners responded to the scolding of Robert Leuchars, an early English authority on hothouses, about maximizing the visual appeal of these structures. The design and influence of these garden additions along the Mississippi were strongly European. It has been only in recent years that some originality and adventure in design have crept in.

Greenhouses and hothouses were not entirely essential in the warm climate of Louisiana and Mississippi, unlike the states further up the country, where people definitely needed them. Greenhouses in the South were more a matter of keeping up with the English tradition of how to do respectable gardening, al-

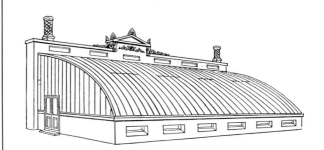

A DESIGN FOR A MID-NINETEENTH-CENTURY GREENHOUSE, TAKEN FROM ROBERT LEUCHARS' 1854 BOOK, PRACTICAL TREATISE ON THE CONSTRUCTION, HEATING, AND VENTILATION OF HOT HOUSES, WITH MARTHA TURNBULL'S NAME AND 1856 INSCRIPTION. POSSIBLY THE DESIGN OF THE ONE AT ROSEDOWN.

THIS SOUTH-FACING HOTHOUSE (CIRCA 1850) WAS USED AT OAKLEY PLANTATION FOR BRINGING ON EARLY CROPS AND BEDDING PLANTS. OAKLEY OCCUPIES A 100-ACRE WOODLAND SETTING NEAR ST. FRANCISVILLE IN WEST FELICIANA PARISH. IT WAS AT OAKLEY THAT JOHN JAMES AUDUBON CREATED SOME OF HIS BIRD MASTERPIECES. THE HEAVY GRANITE ROLLER WAS USED TO COMPACT GARDEN PATHS AND LAWNS.

though to a limited extent, they were needed to protect plants from the occasional frosty nights.

Several plantation owners were following advice meted out by the latest books on how to run the gardens of stately homes. M'Mahon (1819), for example, made these suggestions: "By the aid of hot-bed, defended with frames and glasses, we obtain early cucumbers, in young green fruit, fit to cut or gather in February, March, and April, &c. and ripe melons in May and June."

Along the Mississippi, the greenhouse and hothouse (the terms are actually interchangeable, but greenhouse, for many, indicates a freestanding building of glass) were only required as a safekeeping for frost-sensitive species for approximately three months of the year—from December through January and February at the latest. For this reason these structures tended to be relatively small features in the garden, as they were unnecessary for nine months of the year.

They did nevertheless provide serviceable facilities for several horticulture enterprises. Seeding of vegetables for early plantings was probably their most important function on plantations, where early fruits and vegetables were critical. Propagation of favorite ornamentals and winter protection for species most at risk from frost and needing shelter were ancillary uses. These species included such plants as pineapple, orchids, and bromeliads, as it was very much in vogue to put these sensitive tropicals out on the verandas at the first opportunity for all to see.

The pineapple was, incidentally, a symbol of hospitality, and still shows itself in stone finials on walls, gate pillars, and

THE PINEAPPLE IS A SYMBOL OF WELCOME EVERYWHERE— AND WAS A FAVORITE FRUIT FOR GREENHOUSE CULTIVATION.

other places of special accent in gardens. Of course, it was also a delicious exotic fruit, and one that required some considerable skill to produce because development of fruit takes two years. The glory of pineapple on the table demonstrated the gardener's success at nursing it through the vagaries of the southern climate. The gardeners at Afton Villa, near St. Francisville, grew pineapples in the greenhouse and it is recorded that Susan Woolfolk Barrow, the wife of a wealthy Louisiana planter, David Barrow, grew pineapples in her hothouse on the lowest terrace of their seven-terraced garden. At Rosedown plantation, Martha Turnbull refers to her "pine apples" numerous times in her 1836–95 diary.

As mentioned, from the mid-eighteenth century onward there began a period of enlightenment and enrichment on the use of "exotics" in the garden—on both sides of the Atlantic—and this had its effect on embellishments in the garden. The orangery, the chief landscape structure in many a fine European garden, was in due course to be replaced by conservatories because the plants could be set in soil rather than in pots. Here they received better light throughout the year without having to be moved to outside quarters. Overall growth and performance was superior.

*T*here may have been several orangeries along the Mississippi corridor. Citrus trees, chiefly oranges and lemons, were

THIS "ORANGERY" STRUCTURE IS COVERED WITH PLASTIC TO PROVIDE PROTECTION FOR THE CITRUS DURING THE SHORT, COLD SPELLS IN OTHERWISE MILD WINTERS. (HINES, NEW ORLEANS)

prominent among containerized plants once grown in greenhouses and would be suitably displayed around the garden during most of the year.

Martha Turnbull of Rosedown noted in her May 1845 diary entry: "Set out oranges by the school room—quite cold." Gardeners eagerly awaited that particular time in the spring when the bucketed fruit trees could be wheeled out to benefit from the sun after months of being shut up. It was always a noteworthy event, as John Evelyn in England also recorded in his diary; he was a very keen promoter of the virtues of orangeries. Again in May 1847 Martha Turnbull recorded, "Let out the orangery today." In November 1855 she rejoiced in her success with the tropical fruits: "My orange trees are full of oranges."

Her final entry in the diary gave an inventory of kitchen supplies including fresh fruit. There were twenty-four oranges, presumably grown in the plantation garden. Not only were large quantities of fresh fruits and vegetables needed for the kitchen on the early plantations, but Christmas packages were often sent to family members and friends in distant, colder regions of the country.

Interest in preserving plants during inclement weather is as strong today as ever. People will go to considerable lengths to safeguard tender vegetation during the relatively mild winters, and provide maximum protection to bring through their cherished ornamentals and fruiting plants for the following spring.

A modern interpretation of an orangery is a plastic tunnel, which is simply drawn over a series of hooped fittings on evenings likely to be frosty. It is easy enough to give the plants the air they need on warmer evenings, and they fare much better than if they were in traditional orangeries and wheeled out only at the end of the winter season.

*B*ecause of the intense summer heat, greenhouses, by necessity, are normally emptied of their contents for the warm months. Temperatures exceeding one hundred degrees Fahrenheit are not uncommon during the summer. However, growers of specialty plants such as orchids and bromeliads equip their greenhouses with heating and air-conditioning units and other cooling devices to moderate temperature during all months of the year. While today's buildings do not have the architectural details of those in years past (especially the splendid designs seen in England and Europe), producing plants of all types under glass is a rapidly growing industry along the river. Unfortunately, not only have we lost some structures of architectural quality, but many of the newer greenhouses are not properly designed, ventilated, or equipped for growing plants in this region.

There are many references in early writings to the value of south-facing walls for producing tender plants which needed early morning sun and some protection from light freezes. M'Mahon (1819) advised: "A green-house should generally stand in the

THE BACK WALL AND BASE OF THE OLD GREENHOUSE AT ROSEDOWN HAS NOW BEEN REPLACED BY A SIMPLE BOX PARTERRE GARDEN AND OVERHANGING WISTERIA.

pleasure-ground, and if possible, upon a somewhat elevated and dry spot fronting the south, and where sun has full access from its rising to setting." An 1839 manual by Buist *et al.* instructed gardeners that "the hothouse should stand on a situation naturally dry, and if possible, sheltered from the north-west, and clear from all shade on the south, east and west, so that the sun may at all times act effectually upon the house." Leuchars (1854) confirmed this: "In building a green-house or conservatory, then, light ought to form the first point of importance, as success in plant culture is entirely subservient to it, and we know full well, from experience, that no skill, however, perfect, and no attention, however zealous, will compensate for a deficiency of light."

*T*wo fine examples of garden structures which were used extensively for an assortment of horticulture operations are the hothouses at Rosedown and at Oakley. Similar in design, both are sunken and have south-facing roofs of glass. Plantation owners had a bountiful supply of rotting manure to provide heat for the relatively few nights when temperatures would have dropped below freezing in these subterranean structures. At Oakley there is a manure bin clearly designated inside the hothouse. Cold frames and hothouses were employed for propagation of cuttings, especially those of the favored "Japonicas" (*Camellia japonica*), roses, and Cape jasmine.

Standing on the lawn near the Rosedown hothouse, as it has for more than a hundred years, is an exquisite carved dog—a statue of Martha Turnbull's Irish setter. It is as if the dog is keeping guard over her most prized compartment on the plantation, her propagating structure where she rooted hundreds of cuttings annually. The presence of dog statues is not altogether uncommon in Europe and gives a sense of grandeur.

IT WAS IN THIS HISTORIC HOTHOUSE THAT MARTHA TURNBULL RAISED THOUSANDS OF SEEDLINGS AND CUTTINGS OF CAMELLIAS, MOSS ROSES, AND HYDRANGEAS FOR THE GARDENS OF ROSEDOWN. THE ORNAMENTAL SETTER STANDS GUARD.

At the Cottage Plantation near St. Francisville, there is a rather undistinguished hothouse, not sunken, but with a sloping roof to the the south. Rosedown also has the remains of a south-facing greenhouse (really more of a conservatory), but all that stands is the back wall and the floor area. It was no small operation. A February 1861 entry in Martha Turnbull's diary notes: "We now have 1560 flower pots in greenhouse," and in March 1864 she indicated an even larger inventory of 1617 pots for the greenhouse. Today the back wall of this former greenhouse is resplendent in rampant wisteria and roses and the floor has become a parterre with closely clipped yaupon hedges.

*I*f the hothouse at Rosedown is dignified by its accompanying canine statue, the castellated greenhouse at Dunleith is equally distinguished. The huge columned house itself is about as imposing a dwelling as could be achieved—it is reported to be among the most photographed buildings in America—and the greenhouse, a mere stone's throw away, obviously had to match up to the splendor of the mansion. There cannot be many castellated greenhouses with such a lordly appearance and such ostentatious pretensions anywhere.

Among the most rapidly growing horticulture industries in both Europe and the United States is the pleasure greenhouse business. Gardeners continue to find much delight in growing their favorite plants in these structures. Combined with the other necessary equipment of pleasure gardening like the potting shed,

THIS CONTEMPORARY GREENHOUSE/ CONSERVATORY IS BOTH UTILITARIAN AND COMPLEMENTARY TO ITS GARDEN SETTING. (MORGAN, BATON ROUGE)

soil storage units, and places to keep garden tools and supplies, these workplaces are becoming more carefully designed and integrated into the fabric of the landscape. In times past they were more likely to be freestanding, perhaps screened by plants or fencing, and had little to offer in the way of garden enrichment. But even 150 years ago, the avant garde view was shifting. Buist *et al.* (1839) foresaw the possibilities: "The green-house might be made much more an ornamental object, and could be erected contiguous to the mansion-house, with large folding doors to open at pleasure, and be connected with the drawing-room or parlour." Today, indeed, many are being attached to the house with living quarters opening directly into the conservatory.

Another aspect of European influence is revealed in use of the bell-shaped glass jars and glass "cloches" in early gardens along the Mississippi. In the mild southern climate, these garden protectors provided plants with a considerable advantage over their unprotected neighbors and advanced substantially the date of maturity for plants like cucumber and melons. As M'Mahon directed in 1819, "After sowing the seeds, put on the lights or glasses close; but when the steam from the heat of the bed rises

SCREENED BY A DELIGHTFUL SWATHE OF PERENNIAL FOLIAGES, THIS GREENHOUSE IS PARTIALLY CONCEALED. (PATRICK, BATON ROUGE)

THE SPACE BETWEEN THE PERGOLAS AND THE GREENHOUSE IS RICHLY PLANTED WITH FOLIAGE PLANTS, WHICH GIVE THE IMPRESSION THAT THE AREA IS MUCH LARGER THAN IT IS. (PATRICK, BATON ROUGE)

copiously, give it vent by raising one corner of the upper ends of the lights, half an inch or an inch, which is also necessary in order to prevent any burning tendency from the great heat of the bed in its early state." These bell-shaped structures are still being manufactured in France, albeit in plastic, but at least keeping with the original design pattern.

*G*rand gardens using these protectors can be seen in the illustrations which appeared in Richard Bradley's *The Gentleman and Gardener's Kalendar* published in 1718, copies of which may well have been in circulation at the creation of some of these southern gardens. Dr. amd Mrs. Holden use these antique glass jars in a traditional manner at their authentically created Creole Garden, Maison Chenal, in Pointe Coupee Parish.

One element typical of the noble Englishman's estate which seems not to have been copied in Lousiana and Mississippi is the walled kitchen garden—like the grand one so carefully executed at Mt. Vernon, for instance, which is in a cooler climate. There seemed no need to have this very dominant element—the walled garden—in the garden in the South.

While some plantations no doubt had relatively modest kitchen gardens—as small parcels of land adjacent to the kitchen, as demonstrated at Baton Rouge's Magnolia Mound—others were far more extensive in size and complexity of operations than normally thought. M'Mahon supplies an example of early writings indicating the degree of prominence, the size, and the kind of protection deemed necessary:

FRESH FRUIT, VEGETABLES, AND HERBS WERE GROWN AROUND THE HOUSE AT MAGNOLIA MOUND.

DESIGNED IN THE STYLE OF A CREOLE GARDEN, THIS KITCHEN GARDEN WOULD HAVE SERVED THE SETTLERS' NEED FOR FOOD AND MEDICINE. (HOLDEN, CHENAL)

RAISING A BED WAS AN OLD TRICK IN THE
COLDER AREAS OF ENGLAND TO MAKE THE
SOILS WARM UP A LITTLE EARLIER. ALONG
THE MISSISSIPPI RIVER, WINTER
TEMPERATURES WERE MILDER, BUT RAISING
BEDS ALSO OFFERED EASE OF WORKING AND
WELL-DRAINING SOIL. (ROBIN'S GARDEN,
EMERSON AND ASSOCIATES, BATON ROUGE)

A CONTEMPORARY HERB GARDEN IS NEATLY
PARCELLED OUT TO DIFFERENT HERBS, BUT,
AS IS SO OFTEN THE CASE IN GARDENS ALONG
THE MISSISSIPPI, THE HERBS SOMETIMES
GROW TOO WELL AND OVERWHELM THEIR
ALLOCATED SPACE. (ANDRESSEN, SEVEN
OAKS, KENNER)

The Kitchen-garden is a principal district of garden-ground alloted for the culture of all kinds of esculent herbs and roots for culinary purposes, &c. . . . This may be said to be the most useful and consequential department of gardening; since its products plentifully supply our tables with the necessary support of life; for it is allowed that health depends much on the use of a proper quantity of wholesome vegetables; so that it is of the utmost importance for every person possessed of a due extent of ground, to have a good Kitchen-garden for the supply of his family.

The necessary space of ground proper for a family Kitchen-garden, may be from about a quarter of an acre, or less, to six or eight acres, or more, according to the appropriated limits of ground, the number and demand of the family.

With respect to fences for enclosing the ground, it is most necessary to have an effectual fence of some sort around the Kitchen-garden, both for security of the produce, and to defend tender and early crops from cutting winds. . . . Different sorts of fences are used for enclosing this ground, as walls, palings, and hedges, &c.

*T*he plantation gardens of the southern states were generally burgeoning with the fruits of the forest, and benefited from the importation of tropical fruits through New Orleans and trade up the Mississippi River, reducing the need for walled kitchen gardens. Moreover, as mentioned, sometimes vegetable crops were mixed with the economic mainstays such as cotton, corn, sugar cane, and indigo in the larger plantation fields.

7

Allées and Arbors

Southerners tread the avenues,

breathe the air, and recline under

the trees and arbours of their

paradise, thankfully accepting and

enjoying their glorious boon…

JOSEPH HOLT INGRAHAM • 1835

he grand *allée* of trees leading up to the plantation house set an image which for many constitutes the epitome of southern style. These formal avenues established a special spirit of place, and made guests aware of the social standing of the people they were soon to visit. Nothing could set off an estate better than a majestic, sweeping *allée* of trees leading up to the mansion, with glimpses of the magnificent home between the tree trunks giving a tantalizing view of what was in store. The grandeur of the plantings prepared visitors for the sort of dignified etiquette they might expect upon arrival. There could be no clearer statement of success—and the statement had to be bold in such a flat landscape.

Plantation gardens were constructed during the age of enlightenment in the early to mid-nineteenth century, and the *allées* in front of the plantation houses have a clear European tradition. An *allée* is a straight or curved road or path flanked by a single or double row of trees on either side. Most are designed on a straight axis with the mansion at the terminus. The imposing Louisiana and Mississippi tree-lined avenues have been referred to here as *allées*, although the French may also refer to them as *grande allées* in deserving circumstances.

Southern *allées* are certainly grand in all respects. The visual effect, and the message it conveys, is as good as the entrance drive to many country estates in England. There are also

ONE OF THE MOST FAMOUS VISTAS IN AMERICA, THE EIGHT COLUMNS OF OAK ALLEY (1839) MAKE A FOCAL POINT AT

THE END OF THE FAMOUS SPREAD OF LIVE OAKS, REPUTED TO BE MORE THAN 250 YEARS OLD. (VACHERIE)

emanations of the axial road in Paris, such as those that radiate from the Place de la Concorde, for there was a strong French influence in the southern states and garden designers probably had in mind the formal way of designing gardens. Abroad, especially in England, the *allée* is referred to as a tree-lined avenue leading up to the house, as at Cawke Abbey (Derbyshire) and thousands of smaller country seats. Only about twenty-five years is required for trees like live oaks, planted approximately seventy-five feet apart, to form a distinctive avenue in the southern states. The same effect in England would take at least a century.

*I*n the South, *allées* were invariably constructed between the house and the river, and the view from the house to river was a key focal point. As indicated, the trees matured quickly to become impressive visual elements. Surely among the most note-worthy examples of this design in the region, and the one that has been featured in nearly every reference on plantation life along the Mississippi River, is Oak Alley in St. James Parish, near Vacherie. The stark simplicity of these two-hundred-year-old live oak trees, which control the three-dimensional space around the mansion, is truly among the most photographed views in all America. Another avenue of equal acclaim upriver is Rosedown (St. Francisville). Here thirty-two live oaks, underplanted with azaleas and hydrangeas, arch their limbs much higher to give a

THE MIGHTY MISSISSIPPI PUTS THE PLANTATION HOMES IN SHARP PERSPECTIVE. HERE, OAK ALLEY IS SHROUDED IN ITS LIVE OAKS, WHICH BLEND IN WITH THE MANY OTHER LIVE OAKS ON THE SITE. MANY OF THE LIVE OAKS FOLLOW THE ORIGINAL BOUNDARIES OF THE BIG PLANTATIONS.

OVERLEAF. FESTOONED IN SPANISH MOSS AND COVERED IN RESURRECTION FERN AND IVY, THE LIVE OAKS OF ROSEDOWN.

completely different spatial sensation than that experienced at Oak Alley.

An *allée* laid out in curves is known as a serpentine *allée*, and there is no finer example of this design than at Afton Villa (near St. Francisville). Here the double rows of live oaks planted on either side of the half-mile-long drive are interplanted with towering old azaleas and gardenias. Even after numerous visits, passage down this romantic, moss-draped road always offers a renewed sense of awe and wonder as one eagerly awaits what lies at the end of this grand avenue.

Just a short distance from Afton Villa is The Oaks Plantation, which has an oak avenue with a single curve. The effect of turning toward the house has its own mystery, although there are glimpses of the house before reaching the end of the avenue.

*I*n the grand design of plantation gardens, the *allée* was often the principal axis around which the rest of the plantings were planned. The heavily canopied tree-lined corridors with draping Spanish moss provide such memorable images in many of the South's fine gardens that they were bound to become the inspiration for much writing and the setting for movies through the

THE CONTINUOUS DRIFT OF PINK 'FORMOSA' AZALEAS MAKES AN INVITING ENTRANCE TO THE SERPENTINE OAK ALLEY OF AFTON VILLA (1790-1849). MORE THAN 200 SPANISH-MOSS-DRAPED LIVE OAKS PLANTED IN DOUBLE ROWS FLANK THE ONE-MILE DRIVE TO THE SEVEN TERRACES OF GARDENS.

years. For overall effect, surrounding plantings can have considerable bearing, and grand *allées* have been given greater embellishment in several ways. The edges of some *allées* may be reinforced with walks and mass plantings such as at Rosedown. Here the structure of the lateral enclosure appears to be much tighter than at places like Afton Villa, where the understory plantings are more random and allow open views at right angles to the axis along other junctures within the garden, or to the side spaces such as a woodland glade. One senses more depth in garden spaces where plantings are sometimes broken. At Oak Alley the trees themselves form a much simpler type of enclosure.

The principle of incorporating several axes in gardens is Italian, and this is particularly emphasized when the terrain is terraced, as at the Burn (Natchez), a site rich in geometry and pattern. It is often said that all gardens have axes, whether they are planned or not, but as a garden is essentially an extension of the house, it seems logical to have at least one major axis coming from the house through the length of the garden. Plantation gardens do precisely that with their grand *allées*.

Having an axis accompanied by a gentle change in topography can add immeasurable interest to a garden. The transition from one level to another is best handled by the addition of garden steps if the purpose is to emphasize a grade change, and steps also provide overviews from which one can appreciate the next part of the garden before descending into it.

*T*he trees used principally in *allées* in Louisiana and Mississippi are live oaks, *Quercus virginiana*, since this is a

RICH PLANTINGS OF LIVE OAKS MAKE THIS VIEW FROM THE VERANDA VERY REFRESHING, AND OFFER RELIEF FROM THE SUMMER HEAT. (AMBROSIA PLANTATION, ST. FRANCISVILLE)

native species of remarkable growth rate, longevity, and strength in the fertile Delta soil, and it is a prolific shade provider. Long-lived, with numerous plantings being more than two hundred years old, the live oaks classically bear mammoth, horizontal branches that seem to stretch over the gardens forever. The heavy, gnarled, and twisted shapes are fascinating; each tree has its own distinctive character. The thick, corky bark plays host to the resurrection fern (*Polypodium polypodioides*), which is leafy green following rains and other periods of high humidity. During droughts it takes on dry, near strawlike features, only to be resurrected within hours of a shower.

Many of the live oaks nearest the plantation homes tower over the houses almost protectively. The live oak grows to a height which is normally just a little taller than the plantation home, so that the view from the gallery—in a strategic second-floor position—is into the most intimate parts of the tree. There can be few other such close associations between people and trees.

Gallery viewing at the renowned places like Oak Alley, Houmas House, Oakley House, and Parlange, to name a few, provides close-up views of virtually every wrinkled inch of these trees' nooks and crannies. One can quickly develop a close respect for an individual tree; an arboriculturist's delight. At Parlange (Pointe Coupee Parish) a ladder offers even closer access so that one can venture a climb into the limbs of a two-century-old specimen. Danger might occasionally loom from shed limbs where trees are in such close proximity to buildings, but the charm of the live oaks as pieces of living sculpture is completely irresistible.

Other tree species have been used in *allées*, but on a more limited basis; they are nevertheless important in shaping spaces in garden design. These include the long-lived red cedar (*Juniperus virginiana*), crape myrtle (*Lagerstroemia indica*), and the native pecan tree (*Carya illinoensis*). Rosedown has a mixture of both crape myrtles and cedars. The Louisiana State Capitol grounds in Baton Rouge have probably the finest example of a cedar *allée*. Here two different cultivars of cedar are used to provide contrasting foliage colors which are particularly evident from the observation deck some twenty-four stories above the street.

The flat Delta landscape obviously had an important influence in shaping plantation garden design. One cannot help sensing in the complementary features of the grand *allée* and the gracious home that they were a way to give special definition to plantation life in the monotonously level landscape flanking the Mississippi. If the owners had to live near their work—the cotton, sugar cane, and indigo fields—then something grand had to be erected to counter the low-lying and sometimes swampy surroundings. Nothing would be more prominent than the plantation home, and what could proclaim its stature more effectively than a grand avenue of trees?

DRAPED WITH SPANISH MOSS, THIS CRAPE MYRTLE ALLÉE HAS AN AIR OF MYSTERY AND INTRIGUE. (*LIVE OAK PLANTATION*)

WISTERIA AND BANKSIA ROSE GARLAND THIS PERGOLA, WHICH CONNECTS THE HOUSE WITH THE PIGEONNIER BY WAY OF THE HERB GARDEN. (ANDRESSEN, SEVEN OAKS, KENNER)

This natural evolution toward something that was practical, noble, and elegant seems almost to have been inevitable. And it was repeated many times upriver. The style suited the surroundings, and the opulence must have been keenly felt by both owners and visitors during the carriage ride up the avenues.

*A*rriving in such style would have surely been a fine experience, however long one dallied coming up a serpentine *allée*. The aim of design was to impress, and to incite admiration for as long as possible. A straight *allée* gave some formality and particularly emphasized the house as seen from a distance, but it offered fewer surprises. The curved *allée*—a sophistication not developed widely—gave an impression of traveling through a much larger estate and lent a more informal air to the site. Surprises could be encountered at every bend. If the journey appeared to take a long time, one might imagine a journey through a huge English or German estate, the like of which, no doubt, must have influenced the design of many plantation avenues. The *allée* thus connected the house with the river of prosperity. It was a transition between the two environments, manifesting itself as a zone full of its own delightful qualities. *Allées* make even the more modest plantation houses seem more imposing than those standing in a landscape consisting only of more traditional informal plantings.

As indicated, the importance of the *allée* was bidirectional: it was designed not only to dignify access from the river to the house, but also to form a framed view of elegant proportions for those looking out. Indeed, in skillful examples both perspectives are incorporated quite compatibly. The view along the *allée* was of prime importance for the lady of the house, and the outlook from the upstairs gallery was superior to that from the veranda. At Rosedown, the view down the *allée* from the gallery is among the most impressive vistas in all America. At Longue Vue Gardens in New Orleans there are two avenues. One, along the main driveway, has a view to the entrance court and is framed by closely spaced live oaks with high arching limbs. The other is along the axis of the Spanish Garden, which is dominated by walls and water, with box and wall plantings being somewhat subordinate to the architectural enclosure.

*T*he pivotal point for viewing the garden *allées* and distant scenery was usually the gallery. A late nineteenth-century embellishment of the *allée* in Europe was actually to make the inside of the house the focal point at one end of the *allée*. Near perfection to detail was realized at the Linderhof Castle in the Bavarian mountains. This magnificent structure was created by Ludwig II, with no expense spared. The pivotal point was Ludwig's regal bed, and from this vantage he had a magnificent view up the *allée*: cascading stairs edged in serpentine arbors, and beyond lay countryside stretching away to the alpine mountains in the distance. Kings commonly held court from their beds, and

SLOTTED INTO A SMALL COURTYARD, THIS ARBOR PROVIDES THE ARCHITECTURAL DETAILS AND BACKGROUND FOR A RICH MIXTURE OF SOUTHERN PLANTS. (NEW ORLEANS)

so it made sense to have this point as a basis for an overview through the estate along an *allée*. Plantation owners did not, of course, have access to the inexaustible chancery revenues that Ludwig II had, but the design and elaboration of garden *allées* in the southern states resulted from lessons learned from such assorted European influences. The gallery and the view from the rooms issuing onto the gallery were considered strategic points in the appreciation of the garden.

If the curved *allée* had esthetic and grand intentions, the straight *allée* was strictly formal and directly out of the textbooks of Renaissance Italy. The Mediterranean sun can be so remorselessly hot that shade was often eagerly sought. The long straight *allée* that provided shade was equally effective in the hot climate along the Mississippi River. Instead of tiered terraces leading down the *allée* to the sea, as in Riviera gardens, here the avenues yield welcome shade and relief for the eye on the flat Delta land bordering the river.

*B*ecause southern gardens were often no more than spacious grounds with groves of trees either intentionally planted or carved from the forests, there was a need for a transition in scale from the large, parklike grounds to the more personable, intimate spaces close to the houses. To accomplish this, various types of garden structures were incorporated into the landscapes. In addition to the *pigeonniers*, *garçonnières*, cisterns, and wells which were prominent architectural elements in early gardens along the Mississippi, there were arbors, pergolas, summer houses, pavilions, and other "retreat" buildings. All helped to characterize the southern gardens; to create a sense of opulence, owners relied heavily on such architectural structures to embellish the grounds. While some structures were enclosed and gave protection from the harsh elements (see following chapter), others were typically open and provided a tranquil space where owners and visitors could find peace and solitude in the garden under the protection of vines.

The early landscapes were heavily dominated by nature, for plants were everywhere. As we have seen, to make gardens stand out as special designed spaces, trees and other plants were used in strong geometric pattern and repetition to form avenues and *allées* along carriage and pedestrian ways. Then, within these defined spaces, to provide accent and contrast to the heavy vegetation, garden structures like arbors seemed almost essential as pivotal points of interest around which important segments of the gardens evolved.

These smaller-scaled, intimate structures provided the much needed relief and contrast that no amount of plant materials could give. They also supplied a critical linkage between the various compartments of the garden. These elements punctuated the gardens at strategic points by providing supports for many of the rambling roses and grapes and a host of other popular vines, in addition to giving shelter and shade from the searing hot summer sun.

*I*n a land of hot summers and frequent showers, more substantial types of enclosures were often needed in early gardens. Arbors were among the features of Roman households in Pompeii; in early times the arbors were believed to have consisted of long colonnades covered with plants. More recent vine-covered structures can be seen throughout England and Europe and were the forerunners of today's southern garden shelters. Some southern arbors are relatively simple in design, while others are more elaborate with rich details and strong Victorian influences.

Whatever their design and degree of complexity, all such garden structures were used to set aside a parcel of garden space as separate and distinct from the plant-enclosed "rooms" of the garden. While probably incorporated as much for esthetic purposes as for functional uses, these garden features were ideal for such passive recreational uses as reading, meditation, relaxing, and enjoying tea and other drinks with family and friends in a quiet and secluded part of the garden.

Europeans who first used plants on garden structures in Louisiana and Mississippi perhaps had some rude surprises. Some plants which had a known performance in temperate Europe grew so vigorously as to be almost out of control in the New World. The Lady Banks and Cherokee roses, wisteria, grapes, and

A MASS OF 'GLOIRE DE DIJON' DECORATES THIS TRELLISED GARDEN ARBOR ON THE GROUNDS OF MAGNOLIA HALL, THE LAST OF THE GREAT TOWN HOUSES BUILT IN NATCHEZ BEFORE THE CIVIL WAR. THE "OLD GLORY ROSE" IS A HARDY CLIMBER ORIGINALLY RAISED AS A HYBRID TEA IN 1853.

The tunnel of wisteria at Houmas House is spectacular in mid-March in flower, and forms a heavily shaded path during the summer months. (Burnside)

POLE BEANS MAKE THE QUICK GROWTH AND DENSE FOLIAGE NECESSARY OVER THIS COTTAGE GARDEN ARBOR. VEGETABLES AND ORNAMENTALS ARE COMBINED HERE TO CREATE A DELIGHTFUL SUMMER POTAGER. (GUILLORY, BATON ROUGE)

jessamine grow fifty or more feet within the span of only a few years. At Seven Oaks (Kenner, near New Orleans), a Banksia rose/wisteria arbor skillfully links the *pigeonnier* with the plantation house. At Houmas House, a Banksia rose growing on the *pigeonnier* provides heavy massing, but within keeping at the corner of the formal garden, festooning the hedgerow and trees with blossoms. The fine wisteria arbor at Houmas House is at its best in mid- to late March, but provides a cool, protected covered walk during the summer months. Wisteria and Carolina or yellow jessamine (*Gelsemium sempervirens*), which have been widely planted in southern gardens, have escaped cultivation and naturalized along roadsides, creating magnificent violet-blue and golden yellow swathes which surmount the roadside woodlands and form canopies of draping flowers and foliage, as can be experienced along the bluffs in St. Francisville.

Many other superior traditional vines were selected for arbors and other garden structures, but all have a tendency to grow vigorously and require at least annual pruning to restrain excessive growth. Muscadine or scuppernong grape vine, *Vitis rotundifolia*, was popular for structure cover and summer foliage display as well as providing delicious fruit for the annual jelly and preserve making. A grape-covered arbor also afforded much needed shade during the summer months, but was open and airy in winter. In more recent years, the Confederate jasmine, *Trachelospermum jasminoides*, has gained considerable favor as the vine of choice for many garden structures. Its more refined, evergreen, compact foliage, combined with the highly fragrant flowers, are special attractions.

Many people underestimate the value of certain small tree-form plants, which can provide an overhead canopy that is in essence similar to the enclosure offered by architectural elements. One plant that does this well is the crape myrtle. It is a wonderful performer throughout the South. Some of the lower-growing "weeping" or "umbrella"-type cultivars such as 'Basham's Party Pink,' 'Near East,' 'Seminole,' and 'Pink Lace' give exceptional value when used either alone or in a bosque (grove or close setting) design.

The smooth, satinlike stems of the crape myrtle have a distinct sculptural quality and the plants bloom in pink, lavender, and white, providing special summer color during a three-month period when few other plants are flowering. Spanish moss, *Tillandsia usneoides*, seems to have a preference for the crape myrtle as its host—even more than the live oak—and they make a wonderful complementary pair. At Live Oak (West Feliciana Parish) the crape myrtle *allée* growing adjacent to the house is a distinctive design feature enhancing the eighteenth-century dwelling.

8

Garden Retreats

GAZEBOS AND PERGOLAS

It is thought that Mark Twain wrote

The Adventures of Tom Sawyer

in the refuge of a garden house.

I n nineteeth-century gardens, gazebos and pergolas became a significant garden presence, retreats situated in prominent positions and serving as focal points. Like *allées* and arbors, they provide a transition in size and give the garden a more intimate scale within the larger span of nature.

Historical documents and excavations in Egypt and Italy indicate that garden structures were present by perhaps 3000 B.C. in Egypt in the form of vine-covered trellises. In Renaissance Europe these structures were apparently very fashionable forms of garden embellishment. In fact, the earliest pergolas, or extended arbors, were large enough in width and length for horses to be

ridden in the shade of their cover. Architect Sir Edwin Lutyens, in collaboration with renowned English landscape designer Gertrude Jekyll, frequently designed pergolas into estate gardens. Besides offering private, shaded places for enjoying outdoor pleasures, they were ideal places to exhibit impressive flowering vines and roses.

The word "gazebo" or, less commonly, "gazeebo," is a mid-eighteenth-century word for "I shall see," stemming from the Latin, and meaning either a roof turret commanding an extensive overview, or a special building in the garden. Some authors regard all gazebos as belvederes, but here we are addressing fixed garden structures with the term gazebos. There are many along the Mississippi River corridor, some elevated above ground by a few feet, and almost in the category of a grandstand or garden pavilion.

As a matter of historical correctness, the word "arbour" in its European spelling predates the word gazebo and was used in the sixteenth century. It comes from the old French *herbier* (grass), in turn derived from the Latin *herbarium* (a collection of plants). *Herbier* used to mean a grassy place or lawn, but the now current

A RUSTIC GAZEBO WITH AN ATTRACTIVE COVERING OF MOSSES. CALADIUMS AND COLEUS FORM A DECORATIVE BORDER. (MURRELL, TALLY HO PLANTATION, BAYOU GOULA)

CONTEMPORARY
GAZEBOS DO NOT
ALWAYS HAVE THE
PRESENCE OF
THEIR
PREDECESSORS,
BUT THIS ONE,
SET AMONGST
AZALEAS AND
MULTICOLORED
DIANTHUS, IS A
FINE CENTERPIECE
ON THE GROUNDS
OF THIS HISTORIC
NATCHEZ SITE.
(MONMOUTH)

meaning of an arbor is in the vertical dimension as a trellis or support which can be festooned with plants. Thus the arbor can be a gazebo. Along the Mississippi there are several pergolas or arbors lurking beneath rampant canopies of climbing plants.

Gazebos were invariably placed at critical points in the land-scape where they could be seen from the main dwelling, or where, when occupied, they provided the prime position for viewing into the garden. The design of a gazebo may be square, round, hexagonal or octogonal, with the primary building material in early gardens being brick or wood. Its sides may be open to the elements or partially latticed in attractive styles. In early southern gardens gazebos were generally smaller than *pigeonniers* and *garçonnières*, but soon gained the prominence that these other structures occupied and were often built in the same garden. The affluence of the mid-nineteenth century allowed a diversification of these extravagances.

Some gazebos and arbors may have originated in the grounds of the finest plantation gardens for social needs, since wedding parties and other society events would have spilled over into the garden. A gazebo would serve the dual functions of being an esthetic contribution to the garden and a shelter for visitors from the oppressive heat, or in case of sudden summer rain. It is thought that Mark Twain wrote *The Adventures of Tom Sawyer* in the refuge of a garden house.

Once gazebos were built for a special occasion, their appeal was often so great that they were retained for their elegance and functional values as permanent garden ornaments. They became an important part of the basic plan of the garden, providing a strong contrast in gardens dominated by plants.

Garden designers often consider the space in the garden— the areas of lawn between strong masses of vegetation—as a flowing element. One can journey through a garden via the space which flows comfortably from each part to the next. At some stages in this contrived flowing experience, the eye can be strategically arrested, at a point where a gazebo can be placed. Since attention is naturally drawn to this particular point, the subject will then be much more appreciated. From afar the effect of a structure at the end of a flowing stretch of garden, such as an *allée*, can be most satisfying.

Many of the major garden embellishments in the South were painted white to mirror the decor of the plantation home. White accentuated them, making a social statement that could be seen from afar. Many structures, such as gazebos, pergolas, arbors, and trellises were complementary in design to the main house. They also contrasted well with the lush countryside and the green lawns which were swept and raked, and were sometimes placed adjacent to cool and restful foliages to enhance the outline of the structure.

Two other powerful forces in garden design are the ele-

ROSEDOWN HAS
MANY FINE
GAZEBOS, WHICH
MAKE STRONG
GARDEN
STATEMENTS.

ments of secrecy and surprise. Designers have traditionally aimed to create suspense and wonder about what feature might await one around a corner or down a garden path. Placing structures with care can encourage more adventure, and gazebos served this function well. When arriving unexpectedly at a gazebo, the visitor is likely to stop, and to savor some detail of subtlety that would perhaps be overlooked in a carefree walk through the garden.

In some gardens, several of these "surprise" buildings were strategically placed among lush plantings. For example, Rosedown has three such structures, one being an outstanding example of the hexagon form, with a bell-shaped roof painted the color of brick. The sides are constructed of intricate lattice work, and

THIS GAZEBO AT ROSEDOWN IS STRONGLY MOORISH IN DESIGN.

the building is so placed that there are views along different axes within the main garden. It is situated in the center of the rose garden and is a special feature of this elegant formal garden. The other gazebos, located in the North and South Gardens at Rosedown, are more European and classical in design. Painted white to contrast with the garden vegetation, they become pivotal elements within each garden space. A fourth, much smaller and more modest garden structure at the rear of the mansion signals the division between the formal garden and the woodland garden with its meandering trails. In this case the gazebos serve as important nodes in a garden sequence to indicate significant changes or featured spaces.

*B*oth historic and contemporary garden structures are to be found everywhere along the Mississippi River corridor. Some are old and endearing, while others look a little tired although still carrying romantic overtones, but all are excitingly rich in design and flavor. They contribute to the gardens a particular charm and dignity that plants alone can never provide. An example of a gazebo of classical Victorian design is located in the garden at Tezcuco Plantation at Burnside. Contemporary examples at Monmouth (Natchez) have prominent positions in the new landscape development at this historic house.

At Rosalie (Natchez) the gazebo is upgraded to the status of a small pavilion, for it is built on a substantial brick foundation. Stylistically rich in heavy ironwork, this pavilion stands forlorn in a large meadowlike space. From its slightly elevated foundation,

THERE'S A STRONG VICTORIAN INFLUENCE IN THE DESIGN OF THIS GAZEBO, WHICH ALSO HAS SOME GOTHIC FEATURES. (TEZCUCO PLANTATION, BURNSIDE)

A PROUD REMINDER OF VICTORIAN TIMES, THIS GRAND GAZEBO IS MORE A BELL-SHAPED PAVILION—WHERE NOTABLES COULD ADDRESS A GATHERING, OR WHERE MUSIC COULD BE PLAYED. (ROSALIE, NATCHEZ)

the view over the Mississippi River is among the most notable experiences in this historic town. At Magnolia Mound, the gazebo is a part of the dependency buildings of more contemporary times. It verges upon a pavilion since it has open sides, yet its square pillars, hexagonal base, and curved beams make it a prominent building on the grounds.

If gazebos were a hub around which, and from which, other parts of a garden could be explored, pergolas instead served as connecting structures between one part of the garden or between house and garden. Usually made of wood, and often painted white, they were avenues or arcades which provided shade in the hot climate. A quick dash to the herb garden could be entertained via the pergola, which, in the case at Seven Oaks (Kenner) links the house with the *pigeonnier*, via the herb garden.

*M*ore often than not, early gazebos and pergolas became the support for some of the most fashionable vines and climbing plants of the day. Roses were by far the most popular choices because the climbers would quickly festoon the structures with fragrant blossoms. Other plants noted for their fragrances—

CLAD IN WISTERIA, THIS BOLDLY PILLARED LOGGIA ACTS AS A CENTRAL POINT IN THE GARDEN. MASSES OF PANSIES SURROUND. (MONMOUTH, NATCHEZ)

A LOGGIA IN STYLE; THE CURVES IN THE BRICKWORK AND POOL MIRROR THE CURVED LOGGIA WITH ITS MAJESTIC COLUMNS. (LONGUE VUE GARDENS, NEW ORLEANS)

sweet olive, banana shrub, Carolina sweet shrub, and magnolias—found a welcome home adjacent to these outdoor retreats because the buildings were usually open on the sides, and breezes would waft the scents of the garden through them.

Other vines besides the climbing roses continue to find favor with today's gardeners. These include English ivy, clematis (native and introduced species), wisteria (evergreen and deciduous), Carolina jessamine, flowering maple, and poet's jasmine (*Jasminum officinale*). Because of the rampant growth rate of some of these vines, the "tamer" species are often preferred, especially for structures made of wood. The frequency of maintenance required on wood construction in the region sometimes precludes the use of plants actually attached to the building in favor of the climbers being supported on frames that can be separated from the main structure to allow for periodic maintenance.

IN THE FORM OF ARCHES REMINISCENT OF AN ORANGERY, THIS LOGGIA WAS CONSTRUCTED WITH OLD TIMBERS FROM AN ABANDONED PLANTATION HOME. (TULLIS, NEW ORLEANS)

A SPACIOUS CONTEMPORARY GAZEBO IN NEW ORLEANS. (PITRE, NEW ORLEANS)

How can such buildings be incorporated effectively into gardens today? When used they nearly always become the most featured element in a garden. As in the past, they may be a central focus, with plantings subordinate to the architecture; or, by placing them along a pathway, they can be used to create a surprise for the visitor who ventures into the more "undiscovered" parts of the garden; or they may become focal points at great distances, beckoning the visitor into the garden, and serving to hold the eye within the composition. As indicated, all the above approaches are tastefully used at Rosedown, where some of the finest examples of original structures are well preserved.

*D*esigns vary tremendously. One can choose between making the structure complementary to the architectural form of the house or other buildings on the site, or select a "period" style. Attractive prefabricated buildings are highly promoted in the landscape industry. Once a structure is sited, choices have to be made about whether to paint it—in the more elegant and classical gardens, white is normally the choice and painted buildings are thus highly accented—or to use a more "natural" finish of wood and brick, which will be more recessive and blend into the surroundings.

Plantation gardens of the South would seldom have been complete without their associated collection of pergolas, trellises, and arbors. With much gossip spoken under their fancy roofs, pergolas and gazebos were often the center of attention for the high society which drifted through these charming gardens. Many of today's garden structures are equipped with the latest conveniences, making them attractive and useful throughout the year. The addition of electricity for lighting, ceiling fans to help generate a cooler and more insect-free environment, and water have made many of the modern retreat shelters in southern gardens even more inviting than their predecessors.

THIS WELL-PROPORTIONED LOGGIA HAS FLOOR-TO-CEILING MIRRORS THAT REFLECT THE GARDEN SCENE BACK TO THE VIEWER— MAKING THE GARDEN APPEAR LARGER THAN IT IS. (STRACHAN, NEW ORLEANS)

9

The Joys of Foliage

The possession of quantity

of plants, however good the plants

themselves may be and however

ample their number, does not make

a garden; it only makes a

collection. Having got the plants,

the great thing is to use them

with careful selection and

definite intention.

MARIANA SCHINZ · 1935

he serene quality that pervades southern gardens is a mood created in large measure by the heavy foliage characteristic of the landscapes. The amount of foliage and its refreshing tones impart grace and elegance to southern gardens. When chosen well and used in a creative manner, foliages can be devastatingly beautiful. So it is with many gardens along the Mississippi. The other magic ingredients are warm temperatures, moisture, and light, fertile soil, which all conspire to create a filigree of foliage in a matter of months; similar plantings in other regions of the United States and in Europe might wait a decade to come to perfection.

The dominance of greens in the natural landscape mixes well with the seasonal colors that other plants offer in the garden. Indeed, the native trees and shrubs are the inspiration behind many of the historic plantation gardens as well as contemporary settings. Several plantation gardens are so well integrated into the surrounding countryside that there is no clear division between the grounds and the countryside. From the air this is very apparent, since some plantations are almost impossible to locate among the dark greens of the native flora. It is a mark of the success of designers and gardeners that plantation gardens have blended so well with their surroundings.

The rich, fertile soil is very important along the banks of

THE FOLIAGES REFLECT THE PERFORATED IRONWORK IN

THIS BRIGHT COURTYARD AT THE BURN IN NATCHEZ.

the Mississippi River for plant growth. Although other parts of the South have the same range in temperatures and may even favor a more tropical vegetation, the shallow, dry, infertile soils of other regions somewhat limit the amount of growth without supplementary water and fertilizers. The deep, fertile soils, especially in the Delta region, favor extremely heavy growth. Although there are slight local variations in climate, the fact that the region enjoys a very long growing season results in a heavy, widely diverse flora.

TRADITIONAL CABIN FRAMED IN FOLIAGE. (THE COTTAGE PLANTATION, ST. FRANCISVILLE)

IN A GARDEN OF FOLIAGES, THE BOY, A PIECE PURCHASED IN FLORENCE, SURVEYS A WORLD OF HARMONIOUS TEXTURES AND COLORS. (BURDEN GARDEN, RURAL LIFE MUSEUM)

*G*rowth and change in the landscape are particular characteristics which require the gardener's continual review of plantings and modifications in design. Except for short spurts of heavy flowering in the early spring and rather subdued fall color from the deciduous trees, greens predominate in the South. Even for the highly popular and traditional woody long-lived flowering shrubs such as azalea, spirea, mock orange, rose, and hydrangea, to name but a few, one can expect strong splashes of flower color only for relatively short periods of the year. At other times, the plants are in heavy foliage.

But the thick, green foliages are rich in *moods*. Contrasts and a range of colors emerge as the ever-changing sun plays on different parts of plants, highlighting otherwise hidden attributes. Consider the light playing on the new leaves of azalea, or pouring through the leaves of sassafras, bigleaf magnolia, and silver bell. The greenery was hardly lost on admiring travellers of yesteryear: "...White dwellings, half concealed in foliage," noted one. "A magnificent garden...luxuriant with foliage," and

LIVE OAKS PROVIDE A SPLENDID CANOPY FOR BANANAS AND OTHER TROPICAL SHADE PLANTS SURROUNDING THE VERANDA IN STEELE BURDEN'S GARDEN. (BURDEN GARDEN AND RESEARCH PLANTATION, BATON ROUGE)

A HANGING BASKET OF IMPATIENS LIVENS UP THE DARK UNDERSIDES OF THE LIVE OAKS, OFFERING RICH COLORS THROUGH THE TREES. (DUNLEITH, NATCHEZ)

"dark forests of Louisiana stretching away to infinity in the west." Images of the lush, green landscapes are still those which most people carry away with them after visiting the South.

In this warm, sunny region people usually opt to introduce shade early in their plantings. With rapid growth, the sunny landscapes soon become deeply shrouded in shade. Many home-owners prefer shade and foliages rather than open, sunny land-scapes that favor the more floriferous types of plantings. Shade rules out certain flowering plants such as roses and many of the colorful annuals and perennials. Gardeners often become frus-trated with the maintenance required for their flower and vegeta-ble gardens in the older, well-established landscapes. What might once have been open, sunny spaces have been gradually taken over by tree canopy and shade. The range of plants capable of surviving and giving a show under the canopy of trees is somewhat limited, most being tropical or subtropical species well adapted to the warmer and more humid climates of the world.

*P*lanting options are drastically reduced when light is reduced by fifty to sixty percent. Because tree canopies cover a large part of many southern gardens, plants have to be chosen carefully. In many of these situations turf grasses perform poorly. As the amount of light is reduced, gardeners must choose other groundcover plantings—usually after several attempts with replanting turf. There are groundcovers that can enrich shady

THE VERDANT LEMON GREEN LAWN UNDER THE LIVE OAK CANOPY IS MAINTAINED THROUGH THE WINTER BY OVERSEEDING THE PERMANENT CENTIPEDE LAWN GRASS WITH ANNUAL RYE GRASS IN MID-SEPTEMBER. IT LASTS THROUGH LATE SPRING. (LONGUE VUE GARDENS)

gardens with attractive green mantles, and some of the selections bloom and give color for varying periods. While groundcovers define the ground plain, there are certain foliage plants in shrub form, not necessarily groundcover plants, which provide useful vertical structure in the garden.

The fun and challenge of using foliage plants is a situation which most people face, if not initially in their gardening experiences, at least at some point during their lifetime. The rapid growth and spread of the large trees and shrubs that are the "space formers" always have to be taken into consideration. Foliages offer many unique design features and, when skillfully used, their distinctive textures provide highly contrasting understories to lighten and enrich dark woodlands, making foliage gardens some of our most intriguing outdoor spaces.

The moods of southern gardens change with the seasons. There is a general absence of color during midsummer. Some of this is by design, but much is by default. Gardeners may intentionally choose to feature the cooler colors such as greens, blues, whites, and variegated foliages during the summer months. These more refreshing colors are preferred over the warmer colors of the spectrum like reds, yellows, and browns. During the warm, more stressful months of the year, gardening does not offer the pleasures that it does at other times. Consequently, people rely on the easy-to-grow foliage plants for their major sources of inspiration and seasonal enrichment.

To enjoy a southern garden to the maximum in summer, the most serene elements have always been the cool, refreshing colors of green foliages. Numerous examples can be cited of foliage gardens varied and beautiful in their own right. Nowhere is this better exemplified than at the Burden Garden at the Rural Life Museum (Baton Rouge) where large masses of aspidistra, ferns, rice paper plant, nandina, mahonia, English ivy, liriope, and a wide assortment of low-growing groundcover foliages carry the main spirit of this magnificent setting. It is difficult to believe that green comes naturally in so many shades. And the light reflected off green, shiny foliages can appear silvery or white. Indeed, in Mr. Burden's garden the virtues of light-colored statuary and other garden accessories are particularly enhanced within the special small, foliaged alcoves in which they are so beautifully placed.

The joy of the rich-foliaged groundcover plants is that they can be used in delightful informal drifts. Once established in shade, they are less labor intensive, although they can be among the most demanding types of plantings in full sun because of competition from weeds and grasses. There is no doubt that their structure as understory plantings is of immense value in garden design. The need to escape from the "sun garden" into a foliage garden full of shade has made these plants popular in the South.

Most groundcovers are plants that reproduce vegetatively

THIS LITTLE RESTING PLACE IN THE VERDANT WOODS IS TAKEN BY MERCURY, SEATED ON A DELICATE WELLHEAD. (BURDEN GARDEN, RURAL LIFE MUSEUM)

by divisions and by spreading runners. English ivy (*Hedera helix*) is an old favorite of great renown because of its versatility for allowing plantings such as bulbs, ferns, and other perennials to grow in a harmonious association. In English woods it forms a total groundcover below trees, and may scramble up saplings. Unfortunately, in recent years its use along the Mississippi River has been limited somewhat by a fungus disease to which it appears very susceptible when grown in large areas. The disease is particularly prevalent in the lower Mississippi. English ivy continues to be a groundcover of choice for many gardens upriver in Natchez where the rolling topography ensures better drainage.

Other popular choices are the green-hued tufted liriope (*Liriope muscari*) with its many cultivar selections in single and double lavender and white flowering forms, and the darker green and lower-growing mondo (*Ophiopogon japonicus*). These groundcovers are not just a southern favorite; most are widely used in other parts of the country as well. Mondo can be used as a turf substitute, especially under trees where two-thirds of the light has been filtered out by the canopy. In heavily shaded places it can be used as as unclipped carpet or it may be clipped to a height of two inches to replace lawn turf. Several trailing plants which tend to be somewhat more aggressive in their coverage in this region include trailing periwinkle (*Vinca major*), Asian jasmine (*Trachelospermum asiaticum*), and wedelia (*Wedelia trilobata*).

To a lesser extent, other plants are used in smaller spaces as groundcovers. These include ajuga (*Ajuga reptans*), Japanese ardisia (*Ardisia japonica*), strawberry geranium (*Saxifraga stolonifera*), turkey ivy (*Lysimachia nummularia*), and indigo (*Indigofera kirilowii*). Flowers and berrying are subordinate to the foliage. Ajuga has dark purple-green foliage and blue flowers during the spring, while the strawberry geranium's silvery foliage is most attractive under artificial light and sports tiny white, spiked flowers several inches above the foliage in midspring. Turkey ivy grows probably faster than all of the above mentioned species. Its yellow-green foliage clings closely to the ground with the yellow flowers being also quite close to the carpet of foliage in late spring and summer. Indigo is a deciduous subshrub growing to a height of approximately two feet and features attractive wisterialike flowers in spring and summer, and scattered flowers even into the autumn.

CREEPING OVER EVERYTHING, ENGLISH IVY FORMS A GREEN MANTLE OVER THE RUINS OF THE NINETEENTH-CENTURY GOTHIC MANSION, AFTON VILLA.

A LUSH FRENCH QUARTER BALCONY.

Surely not to be overlooked is the huge assortment of ferns. These are among the South's most noteworthy groups of plants where the foliages are the featured part of the plant. Ferns are particularly attractive in woodland gardens and other naturalistic settings. In ferns alone there is virtually every size and variation in the color green one could desire. The natives make up a sizable list of possible choices. Growing conditions that favor good performance by ferns are moist, fertile soils, fortified with an abundance of humus (decayed plant matter), and ferns require an ample supply of water during the summer months if they are to remain fresh and thrifty.

Masses of the yellow-green marsh or shield fern (*Thelypteris kunthii*) can make a staggering display under the canopy of oaks, pines, and other trees. The strong contrast of dark tree foliages with light green color below provide an attractive display at great distances. Others of special merit include the Christmas fern (*Polystichum acrostichoides*), royal fern (*Osmunda regalis*), sword fern (*Nephrolepis exaltata*), holly leaf fern (*Cyrtomium falcatum*), netted chain fern (*Woodwardia areolata*), cedar or arborvitae fern (*Selaginella* sp.), to name just a few of the many that are well adapted to the region. For smaller plantings of the more tender and delicate species, species frequently used are southern maidenhair fern (*Adiantum Capillus-Veneris*), Japanese painted fern (*Athyrium Goeringianum*), leather leaf fern (*Rumohra adiantiformis*), and Japanese autumn fern (*Dryopteris erythrosora*).

A FRENCH QUARTER WELL SUBMERGED IN TROPICAL FOLIAGE. (GARY WILLIAMS AND R.J. DYKES III)

Longue Vue Gardens in New Orleans is one southern garden where ferns are used extensively among naturalistic plantings in several locations. Here winters are short and temperatures mild, so there is prolific growth from these perennials for most months of the year. In fact, in the lower part of the region, gardeners can get two major flushes of growth annually, especially with the marsh fern. Plantings can be cut back severely in the winter after a heavy freeze, usually in January after the brown foliages become soft and off-colored. Plantings can be cut back less severely in late summer, fertilized heavily, and watered frequently; then the plants will form a fresh flush of new growth within weeks. A few of the ferns are evergreen or nearly evergreen, like the holly fern and the Christmas fern.

Many of the groundcover plants used in the South, including several of the ferns, originated in the Far East—aspidistra, Asian jasmine, mondo, ardisia, liriope, and hosta, for example. The distribution and use of these subtropical plants in the South is prolific. Aspidistra (cast iron) is one of our most versatile groundcovers for deep shade. This plant is well adapted for growth beneath the canopy of both deciduous and evergreen trees. The prominent, broad leaves give a strong-textured quality in shade. Aspidistra will grow in partial sun, but the foliage is normally off-color and the plant becomes unsightly in sunny places.

Hostas, too, are among the most versatile groundcover plants used for their distinctive foliage and flowering in shade.

A GREEN AND WHITE BORDER: THE TALLEST BACKGROUND PLANTS ARE THE WHITE CRAPE MYRTLE, THEN WHITE BUTTERFLY GINGERS, FOLLOWED BY HOSTAS AND GRASSES. (PATRICK, BATON ROUGE)

A MAGNIFICENT CLUMP OF VARIEGATED GINGER (ALPINIA SP.) IS WELL POSITIONED AGAINST THE OPEN BRICK WALL IN A NEW ORLEANS PRIVATE GARDEN. (STRACHAN, NEW ORLEANS)

Although seldom seen growing in large masses, as is typical of plantings in neighboring states further north, hostas are becoming much more widely planted in southern gardens. They are dormant during the winter months, but more than make up for this period of inactivity with their dramatic clusters of foliage in various hues of green, and the welcome surprises of long, spiked flowers which come at various times, depending on species and cultivar selections. Long used in the gardens along the eastern seaboard, and once thought to be intolerant of the hot, humid southern summers, hostas have proven to be well suited to our southern gardens. They are especially well adapted to shady, woodland plantings where soils have been enriched with a generous supply of humus. Unlike many of the other groundcovers, hostas produce a dramatic display of flowers. Two excellent cultivars, 'Honeybells' and 'Royal Standard,' flower on stalks sometimes exceeding three feet during midsummer. There is no doubt that the climate along the Mississippi corridor is fine for hostas. Jon Emerson and Wayne Womack, Baton Rouge landscape architects, grow many species in their suburban gardens.

Certainly not to be overlooked are the other more seasonal groundcovers which add accent color to the otherwise predominantly green garden settings. Caladiums have caught the gardening world by storm, and there are numerous varieties. Their variegated and curvaceous leaves in white and many shades of red and pink with brightly colored veins can be seen at great distances in the garden. The white-foliaged cultivars are particularly effective in dark, shaded places where other colors might be recessive and hardly seen. White selections make a big show at night under artificial light, and are among our most valued summer plants for moonlight nights. Caladiums are frequently used in dark and forbidding woods and as potted specimens on patios and terraces for seasonal color exhibitions.

There are also more upright-growing foliage plants, which make important contributions to structure in foliage gardens. These include fatsia, aucuba, mahonia, podocarpus, rice paper, ginger, banana, acanthus, and elephant ears (*Alocasia* and *Colocasia*).

Parterres and mazes are a fine sophistication of the use of a single species valued for its foliage. A plantation garden without box borders is almost unheard of, and its use is an expression of strong European influence. Parterres or pattern gardens provide an immediate and permanent structure to a garden, setting strong, unifying geometric shapes into the landscape. They can

DRIFTS OF TIGHTLY CLIPPED 'PRIDE OF MOBILE' AZALEAS CARRY THE VIEWER'S EYE FROM THE UPSTAIRS GALLERY TO THE STATUE IN THE DISTANCE. (ROSEDOWN)

be adapted to sites of all sizes and with varying topography, and within the framework of the controlled spaces formed by the box or other plants there is much opportunity for using colorful plants against the contrasting box to soften the strong geometric pattern somewhat.

It is thought that parterres were first used in the sixteenth century by Claude Mollet for Catherine de Medici, the queen of France. The French parterre was modeled after the highly geometric forms of earlier knot garden designs. The first plants used to create these landscape features were the herbs like thyme and hyssop, rosemary and germander. During the seventeenth century, boxwood became the primary plant of choice for outlining parterres. This having long been the method of establishing a control over nature and defining spaces as distinctive garden compartments, it was only logical that early southern settlers, because of their close ties to gardens abroad, chose this method of setting their garden off from the wild world of vegetation surrounding them. And box is reported to have been a possible chemical barrier to the hordes of caterpillars, since boxwood is not attacked by the usual kitchen garden pests.

The predominant plant of choice for parterres now is the Japanese boxwood (*Buxus microphylla*), although the earliest gardens used common privet (*Ligustrum vulgare* or *Ligustrum sinense*) from the Mediterranean in formal geometric patterns. Some native privet was also extensively used in gardens as an alternative or in preference to box, and it came in very useful as a basic hedgerow plant. Probably the finest example of a privet hedge is at the magnificent Creole garden, Maison Chenal (Pointe Coupee Parish). Because of its nearly uncontrollable growth in the region—where pruning is required several times a year—privet was eventually replaced by boxwood.

The first introduction of box into the southern states was English box (*Buxus sempervirens*), but over the years this was not found to be very satisfactory due to the weather, and the more pest-resistant Japanese boxwood took precedence. Today, both species can be found in gardens. Rosedown has original specimens of the English Box (*B. m.* 'Arborescens') planted by Martha Turnbull more than a hundred years ago.

*T*he box parterres at Oak Alley are still laid out in their original pattern, and in New Orleans, the Hermann-Grima House has prim and proper borders of box around its formal, but tiny, courtyard garden. Many of the gardens in New Orleans' Garden District include boxwood to provide formality and pattern in their elegant settings. Longue Vue Gardens in New Orleans also has a pair of neat parterres on either side of its terraces and a much larger parterre along its grand *allée* in the Spanish Court Garden. At Rosedown, the foliage parterres of dwarf yaupon (*Ilex vomitoria* 'Nana') are immaculate and trimmed to military precision several times per year.

Mazes also successfully employ box as a foliage plant, but there are few present-day examples along the Mississippi corridor. The finest one is at Afton Villa but it is a low one—barely three feet tall—and in no way compares with the tall plantings at Hampton Court (Kingston) and Hever Castle (Kent). It has more in common with the low maze in the Elizabethan part of the gardens at Hatfield House (Hertfordshire). Since the original gardens at Afton Villa were designed by a French landscape architect, it is likely that the present maze, designed by Theodore

IMPECCABLE IN STYLE AND MAINTENANCE, THIS BOXWOOD MAZE IS A GREAT REMINDER OF THE FORMAL GARDENS OF FRANCE AND ENGLAND. (AFTON VILLA)

E. Landry, had a strong European influence. Many early designers and architects used basic textbook examples for their design inspiration.

Although the gothic-style house is no longer standing at Afton Villa, the elevated view of the maze is an exciting feature of the garden. Strong lines, beautiful green foliage, and seasonal color provide special interest within this historic garden. The maze is an integral part of the garden design, situated on an upper terrace and part of the general axis leading down the other five terraces.

*T*he English predilection for topiary work in boxwood has apparently never appeared to any great extent in Louisiana and Mississippi gardens. Just about every kind of evergreen shrub has had its day with the pruning shears, being persuaded into fashionable shapes, but for the most part southern gardeners have seemed content with the wonderful yellow-green foliage of the Japanese boxwood, which needs pruning two or three times a year. There now appears to be a renewed interest in these classical pruned forms to create accents in gardens at strategic places. Sales areas at nurseries, garden centers, and other plant outlets offer many different forms for today's gardeners.

One more use of box is in a less formal mode, when plants are allowed to grow naturally without heavy pruning. The old English box grows to a considerable height. Some of the original plantings at Rosedown, for instance, are large and treelike with irregular forms more than twelve feet high, providing a show of foliage as much as a defining pattern.

10

Garden Embellishment

POTS, JARDINIÈRES, AND STATUARY

A garden artist will only use decoration to

heighten the style, that is, the idea from which

his whole construction has sprung. If he incorporates

decorative adjuncts and accessory details,

however picturesque, which are not directly related

to his theme, he will run the risk of diminishing

the creative quality he should be seeking.

RUSSELL PAGE · 1983

here is a school of thought which says that gardens should be able to stand alone without any form of embellishment. The late English garden designer, Russell Page, was quite emphatic about this point: "I consider no modern garden even remotely interesting as a work of art unless it could stand as such, stripped of every single purely decorative attribute."

Few of us would attempt such an exercise, however, and seldom do we visit gardens which we find to be truly stimulating where some type of accessory elements do not play a major role. More often, the criticism is that gardens contain too much ornamentation and that they become busy, with an assortment of

AT THE CENTER OF THE GRAND STAIRCASE AND PATH AT AFTON VILLA IS THIS WONDERFUL

STATUE, SO SERENE IN THE LUSH SURROUNDING FOLIAGE. (ST. FRANCISVILLE)

drifting items out of scale and character with the garden. One landscape architect has characterized this type of overindulgence as a garden becoming "thingy." Yet, in those gardens where special forms of enrichment have been tastefully incorporated into the fabric of the design, we have some of our most memorable experiences.

There is a strong historical precedent for using many different types of ornamentation in garden design. Ornamentation is thought to have been used initially for architectural embellishment in the form of elaborate finials, balustrades, rectangular boxes, cisterns, and other decorative units. Garden embellishment provided transition between the interior and exterior

AGAINST A BACKGROUND OF NANDINA, "PAN" PLAYS INTO AN ANTIQUE LEAD WATER BUTT. BUTTS LIKE THIS WERE FAVORITES IN ENGLISH GARDENS OF THE SEVENTEENTH CENTURY. THIS PIECE WAS DESIGNED BY BRITISH SCULPTOR JOSEPHINE KNOBLOCK. (LONGUE VUE GARDENS)

spaces. The architectural detailing tended to blur the definite lines which often occur today.

Southern garden embellishment has been heavily influenced by European traditions, especially those of the Italians and French. Italian gardens contained a huge assortment of classical mythological figures, and heroes and heroines of national and religious fame, adorning prominent positions. At every turn there were garden focal points depicting gods and notables, and many of these figures still exist as reminders of the role of statuary in early garden design.

*I*t is reported that during the reign of Louis XIV there were as many as 150,000 decorative pots at his beloved Versailles near Paris. Copies of early architectural pieces from across Europe have been reproduced countless times and are offered widely in the landscape industry; articles in current periodicals promote heavy garden ornamentation and catalogues are often most tempting.

In past centuries many garden ornaments in the form of containers, although they appear to have been designed for plantings, were actually not for plants, and plants were frowned upon when first used in conjunction with these early containers.

A pair of lead tubs supports the effervescent growth of the subtropical ixora. The patio overlooks the rose and boxwood parterre. (Longue Vue Gardens)

*JARDINIERE IN A
SOUTH LOUISIANA
CREOLE GARDEN.
(HOLDEN, CHENAL)*

Ancient European gardens and Renaissance estate gardens in Europe and England included containers attractive in themselves, but the overall use of plants was quite restrained. The Chinese, on the other hand, have a rich heritage of growing plants in pots as a means of introducing additional seasonal color to their gardens. Chrysanthemums were among the first plants to be grown in containers for color accent and continue to be used in contemporary gardens, especially during the late months of the year.

Plant containers today are usually best served when the plants are grown to horticultural perfection and the emphasis is taken off the container. "Wistaria [*sic*] branches, or the leaves and starry flowers of a clematis, will make an ornamentation more vivid than scrolls and foliations…" Russell Page implores.

Early English containers were made of "Coade stone," a combination of crushed stone, clay and glass, named after its inventor, Eleanor Coade. When the ingredients were properly proportioned, mixed and fired, this stonelike pottery would last for many years—much longer than terracotta, the primary clay-based material used for making pottery throughout the ages. Nevertheless, terracotta is still the most popular material for container-grown plants. Kilns in Sicily, the location for some of the most attractive designs, have produced gardening pottery for over two thousand years. Terracotta has a relatively short life span, primarily because of its brittle character and the damage caused by freezing temperatures.

*U*nlike in some gardens along the Mediterranean, where plants even today are often subordinate to a rich assortment of garden embellishments, in the South plants will normally be the major component of gardens. Here, the abundance of plant material can sometimes nearly overpower a garden. Accessories are valued as important counterpoints to complete and thus complement the garden, and offer certain qualities which no amount of plants, regardless of how they are used, could ever

A TREE, OR "STANDARD," VARIEGATED HIBISCUS IS BEAUTIFULLY DISPLAYED IN AN ANTIQUE FRENCH JARDINIERE. (LONGUE VUE GARDENS)

fulfill. Ornamentations can thus provide a special charm and personality, and often constitute an accent or focus essential to the overall design, rather than functioning as the term "accessory" might imply.

During the plantation heyday of the mid-nineteenth century, many of the wealthy planters and their wives took great delight in embellishing their gardens with the kind of decorative accessories that they had seen in classical gardens abroad. The most stunning of imported European pots are at Longue Vue. The large orange-green *jardinières* (ornamental containers), which stand nearly four feet tall, were made in a small town called Anduze, one of the gateways to the Cevennes mountains in the Languedoc of France. The company that made these large *jardinières* is still in existence and has been selling this particular design of pottery for more than three hundred years. Those at Longue Vue are some of the earliest and thus are of considerable

SIMPLICITY STRIKES AN ESTHETIC ACCORD: THE SIGHT LINES PASS ALONG THE BOX BORDER TO FOCUS ATTENTION ON THE DELIGHTFUL OLD JARDINIERE. (ELMS COURT, NATCHEZ)

historical importance in the annals of garden design. Their rich mottled blend of green and orange harmonizes with all sorts of plants grown around them. Another pot of similar vintage, likewise imported purely for garden design, can be found at Maison Chenal.

Some of the plantation garden containers, seen today as reproductions widely used in gardens, were all too familiar a sight along the Mississippi River. With the river so close and being the primary artery of transportation, most of the mainstay supplies not produced on the plantation were transported on river boats in large containers. For example, olive oil and spices came in *olla* pots or jars and were locally placed in smaller bottles for resale and distribution. Demijohns brought French wines to Louisiana and Mississippi tables. At Elms Court (Natchez) there are fine pots displayed outside the house and these probably had a previous life trading olives or dried fish across the Atlantic and the Mediterranean. Today we see a revival in the use of some of these nicely proportioned containers in gardens.

The gathering of European statuary of quality for the Mississippi corridor gardens was also widespread in the past. Rosedown, Longue Vue, Houmas House, and Burden Garden at

A DISPLAY OF ROSES AND BOX PARTERRE IS ENCLOSED BY A PLANTING OF CRAPE MYRTLES AND OLD CAMELLIAS. GROWTH IS SO PROLIFIC THAT CONTINUAL CLIPPING AND PRUNING IS ESSENTIAL. (ROSEDOWN)

LIKE A LAVENDER WATERFALL, THE CHINESE WISTERIA POURS OVER THE BACK WALL OF THE OLD GREENHOUSE TO FORM A BEAUTIFUL SETTING FOR THIS STATUE OF "EVE." (ROSEDOWN)

the Rural Life Museum in Baton Rouge can all boast nineteenth-century pieces disposed in distinguished positions, and at Steele Burden's private garden old European favorites are still being collected. Burden's garden has very intimate, esthetic collections of pieces of a more informal nature displayed throughout the garden.

In 1851, Sara Turnbull traveled to Europe to visit the classic gardens and shop for garden statuary. In Florence, she and her parents selected fine pieces for Rosedown at the firm of F. Leopold Pisani. The massive items were transported by ship to the United States and arrived in 1852 at Bayou Sarah (a settlement which was to become the largest river port between Natchez and New Orleans), where they were placed on ox-drawn carts to be moved to their permanent homes along the live oak *allée* in Martha Turnbull's beloved West Feliciana garden, Rosedown.

*T*ypically in Italianate gardens, statuary is displayed to great effect in borders backed with dark foliage. The statuary is invariably white or grey. The pieces are very good at accentuating an otherwise monochromatic area of the garden, such as a leafy corner. A lot of useful design effects can be gained from a little embellishment such as a pot or statue. Regardless of size, judicious positioning of a garden ornament is important in the overall scheme; and depending on the object, it can be used to sweeten, soften, or to stiffen design features.

SET AGAINST THE DARK VOID BENEATH CAMELLIAS, THIS EASTERN LADY MAKES A STRONG ACCENT OVER A BORDER OF WAX BEGONIAS, BOX, AND LIRIOPE. (STRACHAN, NEW ORLEANS)

Garden statuary functions effectively to enhance views, or "pull" the not-quite-committed visitor into a more intimate relationship with the pleasures of a more distant part of a garden. Statuary frequently "closes" the view and thus terminates a featured part of a garden. While proportion and scale are critical design criteria for the effective use of garden statuary, it only takes a modest introduction to make a strong impact.

Owners of fine gardens along the Mississippi River continue to invest in fine garden statuary. At Afton Villa, the Trimbles added four larger-than-lifesize figures in the forecourt of the Ruins Garden soon after acquiring the property in 1972. More recently, statues of four children, each playing a different instrument, were beautifully positioned on the edge of the woodland under the sprawling canopies of two century-old live oaks. Great characters of mythology and Greek gods and goddesses continue to be reproduced in various sizes to suit nearly every taste, size of garden, or mood that one wishes to convey. They become the powerful, eye-catching images around which a garden space evolves to provide a setting for thought and conversation.

*T*rade with Europe was responsible for many more garden accessories besides containers and statues ending up in Louisiana and Mississippi. Greenhouses were imported in flat-packs, and seats and benches also made their way to the Mississippi corridor from across the Atlantic.

Garden furniture can provide some of the most significant accents in gardens. Being highly functional, furniture in the form of benches, chairs, and other types of seating establishes a particular scale relationship which no other garden object can do. Associated with seating is the invitation to come and participate in the ambience of the place. Whether painted white as points of

ONE OF THE FOUR MUSICAL CHERUB FIGURES AT AFTON VILLA.

A BENCH INVITES VISITORS TO STAY AWHILE IN THIS COUNTRY GARDEN. IT IS SURROUNDED BY RESURRECTION FERN, MOSSES, AND ASPLENIUM FERN. (TALLY HO PLANTATION, BAYOU GOULA)

high accents or more muted presences of natural wood, cast iron, stone, or concrete, they help to set a mood for intimacy and contemplation within a garden setting.

As has been emphasized, the position of ornamental pieces such as statues, pots, and *jardinières* in the garden is always important. Any form affects the mass and void of a garden and gives off its own tensions and vibrations wherever it is placed. Such is the skill of positioning garden ornaments that the disposition of a single pot can enhance that part of the garden to good effect. When the tensions set up by adjacent foliage are not cramped or muted, the object can be most effective as a single item. The eye focuses much more readily on a single piece than on a pair, which suggest a more formal design.

Many Mississippi corridor gardens display Italianate features in which pairs of pots or statues enhance terracework. At Afton Villa and The Burn (Natchez), on descending the terraces while surveying the scene, the tendency is to look ahead; but there are exceptions. Occasionally, embellishments are at the foot of each terrace on either side of the flights of steps, but *below* them, so that they are not seen while descending. This is a means of creating interest at the bases of the terraces which can only be appreciated by turning around and looking back up the *allée*—a

A LARGE JARDINIERE IS PERFECTLY IN SYNC WITH THE COLUMNS OF SEVEN OAKS, KENNER.

THE BURN, NATCHEZ.

grand surprise. The flat Mississippi Delta is hardly conducive to tiered Italianate gardens, and those that have opted for that choice are never very steep. The steepest in the region is probably at The Burn in Natchez.

Gardens which are genuinely Italianate in design, plantings, and embellishments, are clearly different from gardens which merely have a lot of statuary and other embellishments. Sometimes the overall impression of richly ornamented gardens is indeed one of being cluttered and without any coherent theme. In other words, the use of embellishments can go wrong, as Russell Page warns.

It is easier to avoid going awry using only container-grown plants for ornamentation. In true Jekyllian style, moods and tastes of gardens can be changed instantaneously by shifting and relocating plants. This capitalizes on the plant material available at any given time and shows plants off at their best in interesting combinations. Though the effect is transitory, it does offer the possibility of remolding the garden structure in a temporary manner while not interfering with the dominant garden style.

There has always been a deep-seated love for growing plants in the South. While not everyone has the desire or oppor-

REPOSING IN A SMALL ENTRANCE COURT, THIS LADY IS ACCOMPANIED BY SPIDER PLANT, IMPATIENS, CALADIUMS, AND MAIDENHAIR FERN. (MAGEE, BATON ROUGE)

tunity to have a parcel of land or to make an impressive garden, most people grow plants in some fashion, and interest in container plants is flourishing. With the strong competition among commercial growers, their ability to mass-produce plants in a fraction of the time required in earlier days, and hence the greatly expanded assortment of plants being offered, gardeners are enjoying ever increasing opportunities for garden enrichment from container-grown plants.

The seasonal changes of species in the pots give an added expression of originality and many possibilities. One is able to imprint a personality, to register a certain charm on the garden, and to change moods. Even common plants used in unconventional ways, such as growing in a container, take on a different meaning than when part of a planting in a bed. Exhibited in a container of their own, they become immediately important as featured materials. Plants which are pruned and made to grow in a particular form, such as one of the many topiary forms, become even more highly accented elements.

*T*hrough the years, poachers, vandals, and curiosity seekers have stripped many old gardens of everything that could be removed from the premises. Today, there are precious few

"EVE," BY HIRAM POWERS, FAMOUS AMERICAN SCULPTOR. (HOUMAS HOUSE, BURNSIDE)

reminders of the fine old imports. Excavated fragments or pieces lurking in the most remote parts of the gardens evoke more extravagant days. Along the Mississippi, there is also a certain amount of what one might call "passive gardening," which is without any real attempt at introducing embellishments. This laid-back, easy-going southern style of gardening imparts a serene nature to some properties and can be a blessing in disguise. It may even offer more enchanting and wistful moments than many a contemporary designer garden with all the trimmings.

Apollo, an 1850's piece, has plenty of time to think in this secluded woodland glade. (Burden Garden, Rural Life Museum)

11

The Pleasure Garden

I hold that the best purpose

of a garden is to give delight

and to give refreshment of

mind, to soothe, to refine and

to lift up the heart in a spirit

of praise and thankfulness.

GERTRUDE JEKYLL

ardening is alive and flourishing along the Mississippi River corridor. Throughout history gardeners have had their own interpretations about how things should be and they have added numerous layers to the foundations of the past. The resurgence of interest is being demonstrated in ways ranging from small, modest developments to the more extensive reconstruction projects taking place on many plantations as well as in urban centers. Organizations like the Southern Garden Symposium, the Foundation for Historical Louisiana, the Southern Garden History Society, the many pilgrimage organizations, plant societies, and garden clubs are recognizing and promoting the work of many individuals and groups who enjoy gardening and want to preserve the garden heritage of the region. This chapter focuses on the wide assortment of pleasure gardens which occur near the river. Borrowing and adapting from the past, gardeners continue to find immeasurable joy and satisfaction working with and controlling nature.

Gardens of the region can be divided roughly into five types. First, wild gardens, the untamed settings where virtually no changes have been made to the habitat and where indigenous plants of the region go through their unique natural processes and

MANY A LOUISIANA ROCKING CHAIR HAS SEEN TIME PASS BY. MRS. U. B. "JO" EVANS HELD COURT IN THIS CHAIR UNTIL MID-1991 (DURING THE WRITING OF THIS BOOK, IN FACT), WHEN, TWO MONTHS AFTER THIS PHOTOGRAPH WAS TAKEN, SHE DIED IN HER 92ND YEAR. PLANTS FROM THIS PLANTSWOMAN'S HANDS WERE RENOWNED THROUGHOUT LOUISIANA AND MISSISSIPPI, AND USED FOR THE NATCHEZ PILGRIMAGES. (HAPHAZARD PLANTATION, FERRIDAY, LOUISIANA)

nature is celebrated "in the raw." Second, naturalistic gardens, where some clearings and underplantings have taken place, but where indigenous species are dominant and introduced species are limited in number. Here there is ample room for plant spontaneity and lots of growth takes place, eliminating the need for—and intensifying the impact of—other species. Third, the semiformal gardens, where evidence of design structure and boundaries are set forth in both planting and architectural materials which make for a rather definite "footprint," but natural processes are still given considerable freedom. Fourth, formal gardens, where almost total control of plantings and architectural materials is used to form a highly defined, structured space. And finally, the theme or specialty gardens, highly influenced by a monoculture or single species planting such as roses, camellias, or daylilies. Other specialty gardens may include themes like color gardens (white, yellow, etc.), vegetable gardens, herb gardens, wildflower gardens, butterfly gardens, and water gardens.

*T*oday there appears to be a trend toward a more casual and relaxed attitude about gardening. Rather than holding onto age-old stereotypes which conjure certain traditional images that

A DELIGHTFUL SEATING AREA IN THE SHADE, WITH 'GEORGE C. TABER' AZALEAS, FATSIA, AND VARIEGATED ASPIDISTRA. (ANDRESSEN, SEVEN OAKS, KENNER)

THE SOFT LINES AND GENTLE GREENS IN THIS SUBURBAN GARDEN ARE CHARACTERISTIC OF THE "NEW" GARDEN STYLE. (PATRICK, BATON ROUGE)

MOUNDS OF LANTANA CASCADE OVER THE POOL, NOW A STAPLE IN MANY CONTEMPORARY GARDENS, IN THIS GRAND NEW ORLEANS GARDEN.

require rather specific management practices, gardeners are experimenting more and developing the home grounds in a style that better reflects personal desires and lifestyles at a particular time. Young homemakers are approaching outdoor spaces very much the way they relate to the interiors of their homes— making the entire place a comfortable, relaxed, inviting space for family and friends. Unlike interior spaces, gardens are always changing, never static, and the style which might have provided a happy experience at one time may be totally out of character and unsatisfying a few years later.

Responding to the multiple factors influencing design style, today's gardeners appear to be more discriminating and are responding to personal desires and the natural system in search of a garden solution that meets their unique needs. They no longer want to be slaves to the high-maintenance landscapes of their ancestors or to have a place just like their neighbor's, but prefer to identify and celebrate their own garden identity. The site and its surroundings are allowed more influence on the final character of the landscape. Management practices are likewise less stringent. While there is still conscious maintenance required to provide the necessary boundaries, the overall appearance of many contemporary gardens is strikingly different from the structured look of the past. Unfortunately, the temptation to purchase plants without really assessing eventual objectives sometimes entraps people, so that they purchase and plant and continue to "decorate" without an overall theme or scheme.

With the exception of most in New Orleans and some in Baton Rouge, gardens in the region are generally quite large by most standards. Although present-day plantation sites along the river may be only a fraction of the vast landholdings of the nineteenth century, they are still large, containing multiple acreage with the gardens themselves occupying only a small fraction of the total area. These spaces are ripe for expansion and restoration to the spirit that guided their mid-nineteenth-century glories. The visual, tactile, and aromatic pleasures of the last century continue to inspire gardeners as we experience a renewal in gardening along the river corridor.

Throughout this book we have shown vignettes of different types of gardens, principally large plantation gardens, interspersed with smaller, more private gardens. And from this ensemble has emerged a general picture of the contemporary garden, its major characteristic being a more casual and naturalistic approach. These informal contemporary gardens are geared for lower maintenance, although they may involve a lot of construction in their initial fabrication, and are often full of detailing. Gone are the days of the large formal pleasure gardens along the banks of the Mississippi, which required extensive labor to clip every blade of grass, sweep every leaf, and prune every disorderly bunch of leaves.

Another more contemporary attribute is the emergence of a strong feeling of stewardship toward the land, the hallmark of a more caring society. This is expressed in a more considered way of gardening which weighs the environment and the growing condi-

PERFECT MATES: A PICKET FENCE AND LARGE PHILIPPINE LILIES (LILIUM PHILIPPINENSE) IN A CENTER-CITY PERENNIAL GARDEN. (EMERSON AND ASSOCIATES, BATON ROUGE)

A LUTYENS SEAT AND 'BASHAM PARTY PINK' CRAPE MYRTLE. NOTE THE CISTERN IN THE BACKGROUND. (ALMA PLANTATION, LAKELAND)

tions of different plants. There are more people protective of, and showing a greater responsibility for, the conservation of their landscape with a reduction in the use of environmentally harmful chemicals in the form of herbicides and pesticides. There are many more gardens now along the Mississippi corridor which demonstrate a lot of enthusiasm and love for simple horticulture and gardening pleasures.

Related to this, there is a popular trend today to attract wildlife to the garden, especially songbirds. As far back as the sixteenth and seventeenth centuries, birds, most often pigeons, were enticed to the grounds and given shelter and food in elaborate dovecotes, but for rather utilitarian reasons—primarily for food. Today, with natural forest habitats being reduced at an alarming rate and replaced with monoculture and urban developments, the garden is rapidly becoming a haven for many birds. Their presence adds a special charm and animation to the garden; glimpses of darting birds attract our attention and focus our thoughts on the natural garden environs.

*W*hile the big dovecotes of yesterday are now used mostly for ornamentation, elaborate birdhouses, feeding stations,

and sources of water in the form of garden pools are being added to contemporary gardens. There is considerable interest in introducing plants to attract birds, notably indigenous fruiting species. Birds that have a safe, chemical-free environment where they can find shelter, food, and seclusion for nesting provide welcome forms of garden pleasures. Bird watching is second only to gardening as a favorite American pastime, but increasingly the two are combined to add a special dimension to the gardening experiences.

The size of the garden has little bearing on its esthetics. In today's smaller gardens, small can be very meaningful, as we can experience in many urban gardens. Just as the trend has been to make a tiny side yard into a garden suitable to the needs of western living, so there has been an enthusiasm for making the most of the limited "ordinary" gardens in the southern states. An important constraint on the contemporary garden is that there are now many busy, fast-moving people who want a picture garden with instant payoffs. They need to touch base with nature every day, their green garden, their private yards, back, front or side, and they have an insatiable appetite for beautification in the home garden.

SPRING PHLOX, ALWAYS A FAVORITE IN OLD GARDENS, CREATES QUITE A SPECTACLE WITH ITS BRIGHT FLUSHES OF COLOR. IT GROWS WELL IN SUN TO PARTIAL SHADE. (AFTON VILLA)

NATIVE AND INTRODUCED SPECIES IN A NATURALISTIC URBAN GARDEN. (EMERSON AND WOMACK, BATON ROUGE. COURTESY FINE GARDENING)

Another change in the design of suburban gardens that reflects the lifestyle of the modern world is the shift away from the typical American front yard, which for decades has been stereotyped as a formal lawn and a few shrubs with a tree or two. Instead this space is now becoming the area to place a private garden or even a swimming pool, a move which would once have been incomprehensible. The formal lawn is then replaced with informal flower beds. Gardening out front is changing the temperament and mood of many neighborhoods, and giving a refreshing look to typical U.S. residential sites.

Some aspects of gardening in the South have changed little. We are still dabbling and experimenting with exciting new introductions of plants, asking the same questions that settlers asked two hundred years ago about how best to grow introduced species, how to cultivate our favorites, and to learn more about the latest techniques in propagation. Many of the horticultural and pest control questions have hardly changed.

Similarly, the phenomenal growth rate of plants in this part of the South, which makes gardening so pleasurable, is a dynamic constant. Growth is fundamental to an understanding of the region's gardens, and how the fabric of each garden is shaped.

IN THIS SMALL NEW ORLEANS COURTYARD A SENSE OF PLACE HAS BEEN ESTABLISHED, WITH LARGE TREES PROVIDING THE VERTICAL FEATURES AND CALADIUMS, GINGERS, AND FERNS CONTRIBUTING TO THE GROUND LEVEL DETAILS. (HOTEL PLACE D'ARMES, NEW ORLEANS)

Gardeners from elsewhere often get a rude horticultural shock over the rapid growth of plants here. Others who move into the region become frustrated and cannot handle the green explosion in their own backyards; dealing with somewhat "static" gardens of other places is relatively simple in comparison with managing the rapid plant growth of gardens along the Mississippi.

This growth is chiefly due to the quality of the soil and long growing seasons. Even in Florida, which has similar hot and humid climatic conditions, the growth of plants is not the same. The nutrient-rich and nutrient-replenishing alluvial soils of the Mississippi Delta is the vital ingredient. And the impact on gardens is that change occurs much faster than anywhere else in America. Cuttings a foot tall in the spring can grow to eight feet by the end of the year. After one year heavy pruning, thinning, and cutting back is required if the garden is not to revert to a free-for-all where survival of the fittest is the order of the day. Hedgerows often need to be clipped at least six times a year; twice the rate for a privet hedge in England. If you can restrain the plants, the right ones, the pleasures can be yours in profusion.

*O*ne key to the successful pleasure garden is consideration of the importance of ecological constraints. Students in land-

GREEN LEAVES, NATCHEZ.

REFLECTING THE NEW TREND IN GARDENING DESIGN: A LARGE QUANTITY OF PERENNIALS IN A SMALL PLANTING AREA. (GILL, NEW ORLEANS)

scape architecture at Louisiana State University are involved in local projects where they have produced very sympathetic plantings in private as well as public gardens. In the case of public green spaces it is perhaps not widely known that the results of comprehensive surveys of socioeconomic groups are blended with the ethnic tastes of residents before any plantings are commenced, and this is all done on a sound ecological basis of what plants will grow best in particular soils. Neighborhood beautification and urban plantings affect the mood and character of a community for a very long time, and it is pleasing to see such effort being devoted to developing sound plantings.

Not to be overlooked in an overview of gardening in the region are the vegetable gardens, specialty gardens which afford some people considerable pleasure. Many find their greatest delights in vegetables because they can grow the kinds they prefer under conditions without pesticides. In the early days this garden operation was an essential component of the plantation complex, not a matter of pleasure or pastime. Today, while seldom perceived as a necessity, modest vegetable plantings are being integrated into the fabric of the total landscape scheme.

The concept of *potager*, or an ornamental vegetable

AN EXUBERANT BATON ROUGE COTTAGE GARDEN. (CABALLERO, BATON ROUGE)

garden, is becoming more widespread. Here all types of plants—vegetables, herbs, and ornamentals are grown as one—providing plants for cut flowers, food, and the culinary spices. Some people are adding small touches of vegetables and herbs to their flower beds and other plantings. With abundant fresh produce in stores, and reduced interest in canning, preserving, and freezing, purely utilitarian vegetable growing has declined. But even small gardens can, under good management practices, produce a bounty of vegetables for today's families.

We do not imply that contemporary gardens are the best; we simply offer a range of contemporary gardens to illustrate how gardening is progressing along the Mississippi River corridor. In the search for originality, one returns to the distinctive charm of plantation gardens set beneath romantic live oaks. They were created during a completely different age, under circumstances now gone, and what is left today is but a vestige of that era. The high life of plantation owners was of a different order from most people's lives today, analogous to the gracious style on the grand estates of Europe, the stately homes of England, or the châteaus of France: the quality of the gardens emphasized the stature of their masters. What is left of the grand Mississippi corridor gardens today should be conserved for the historical garden record.

Garden styles will continue to be borrowed and adapted to the whims of garden entrepreneurs. Along the Mississippi River corridor nearly all the world's garden styles can be found. There are perfectionists' gardens—quite a lot—and there are eclectic gardens which suit other tastes. Gardens were and are constructed for or by a particular individual, and exude personal expression.

We, as outsiders, as visitors, are privileged to venture inside to reconnoiter the area for a short while, and to imbue the romance and subtleties enclosed within. We may get the nuances wrong, and we may not always see the garden from the inside out, as another room of the house, so that we may miss some perspectives on it. However, we continue to enjoy other people's gardens, and to enjoy the latest trends, if not try them out ourselves. The grandeur and elegance of a past era may have been lost forever, like the water that flows past the entrance to so many of the Mississippi River plantations, but we can learn from those gardeners, and create our own pleasure gardens at home in our own style.

No occupation is so delightful to

me as the culture of the earth, and no

culture comparable to that of the

garden. I am still devoted to

the garden. But though an old man,

I am but a young gardener.

THOMAS JEFFERSON • 1811

Bibliography

Alexander, Rosemary, and Anthony D. Pasley. *The English Gardening School: A Complete Course on Garden Planning and Design.* London: Michael Joseph, 1987.

Bailey, L. H. and Ethel Zoe Bailey. *Hortus Third.* Revised and expanded by the staff of the Liberty Hyde Bailey Hortorium. New York: Macmillan Publishing Company, 1976.

Berrall, J. S. *The Garden.* London: Thames and Hudson, 1966.

Boisett, Caroline. *Vertical Gardening.* New York: Weidenfeld & Nicholson, 1988.

Bradley, Richard. *The Gentlemen and Gardener's Kalendar.* 1718.

Brooklyn Botanic Garden. *Origins of American Horticulture: A Handbook.*

Bridgeman, T. *The Young Gardener's Assistant.* New York, 1840.

Brown, Susan. *Home Topics.* Troy, New York: H. B. Nims and Company, 1881.

Buchan, William. *Domestic Medicine.* 1828.

Buist, Robert, E. L. Carey, and H. Hart. *The American Garden Directory.* Philadelphia, 1839.

Coates, Peter. *Great Gardens.* London: Weidenfeld & Nicholson, 1963.

Costa, Margaret. *Four Seasons Cookery Book.* London: Sphere, 1976.

Cuming, Fortescue. *Sketches of a Tour to the Western Country.* Pittsburg, 1810.

Cruickshank, Helen G. *William Bartram in Florida 1774: The Adventures of the Great American Naturalist, Explorer, Artist.* Sponsored by the Florida Federation of Garden Clubs, Inc, 1986.

Dictionary of Architecture and Building.

Feltwell, John. *The Naturalist's Garden.* Topsfield, Massachusetts: Salem House, 1987.

Feltwell, John. *American Gardens in Style.* (In press.)

Final report and recommendations, special task force on the care of the state capitol grounds. Baton Rouge: State of Louisiana, 1987.

Foley, D. J. *Garden Ornaments, Complements and Accessories.* New York: Crown, 1972.

Hadfield, Miles. *Topiary and Ornamental Hedges.* London: A & C Black, 1971.

Hamilton, Anne Butler. *A Tourist's Guide to West Feliciana Parish: A Little Bit of Heaven Right Here on Earth.* New Orleans: Habersham Corporation, 1983.

Henderson, Peter. *Gardening for Profit: A Guide to the Successful Cultivation of the Market and Family Garden.* New York: Orange and Judd Company, 1967.

Hoskings, W. G. *The Making of the English Landscape.* London: Penguin, 1955.

Hunt, Peter. *The Book of Garden Ornaments.* London: Dent, 1974.

Hunt, John Dixon, and Peter Willis. *The Genius of the Place: The English Landscaped Garden 1620–1820.* Cambridge, Massachusetts: M.I.T. Press, 1988.

Ingraham, Joseph Holt. *The South-west by a Yankee.* Readex Microprint Corporation, 1966.

Jeykll, Gertrude, and Edward Mawley. *Roses.* London: Penguin, 1984. Original title, *Roses for English Gardens.*

Jeykll, Gertrude. *Colour Schemes for the Flower Garden.* Woodbridge, Suffolk: Antique Collectors Club, 1982.

Jones, Katharine M. *The Plantation South.* New York: Bobbs-Merrill.

Kane, Harnett T. *Plantation Parade.* New York: William Morrow and Company, 1945.

Lane, Mills. *Architecture of the Old South: Louisiana.* New York: Abbeville Press, 1990.

Lane, Mills. *Architecture of the Old South: Mississippi and Alabama.* New York: Abbeville Press, 1989.

Letellier, Dominique. *Pigeonniers de France, Histoire Economique et Sociale Technique Architectural, Conseils et Restauration.* Toulouse: Privat, 1991.

Leuchars, Robert B. *Practical Treatise on the Construction, Heating, and Ventilation of Hothouses, Including Con-*

servatories, Glass-houses, Graperies, and Other Kinds of Horticultural Structures. Boston: John P. Jewett & Company, 1854.

Lockwood, Alice G. B. *Gardens of Colony and State, Gardens and Gardeners of the American Colonies and of the Republic Before 1840*. New York: Published for the Garden Club of America by Charles Scribner's Sons, 1934.

Loudon, Mrs. *Guide for Ladies and Companion to the Flower Garden*. New York: Wiley, 1855.

Loudon, John Julius. *Sketches of Curvilinear Hothouses*. 1818.

Odenwald, Neil, and J. R. Turner. *Identification, Selection, and Use of Southern Plants for Landscape Design*. Baton Rouge: Claitor's Publishing Division, 1987.

Overdyke, Darrell. *Louisiana Plantation Homes*. New York: American Legacy Press, 1981.

Magnolia Mound Plantation Kitchen Book. Baton Rouge: Magnolia Mound Plantation House, 1986.

Malone, Paul, and Lee Malone. *The Majesty of the Felicianas*. Gretna, Louisiana: Pelican Publishing Company, 1989.

M'Mahon, Bernard. *The American Gardener's Calender*. Philadelphia: 1819.

Nicolson, P. *Vita Sackville-West's Garden Book*. Fallbrook, California: Futura Publications, Ltd., 1968.

Page, Russell. *The Education of a Gardener*. New York: Random House, 1983.

Ripley, Eliza C. *Social Life in Old New Orleans*. New York: Ayer Company Publishers, 1912.

Rose, Graham. *The Traditional Garden Book: The Complete Practical Guide to Recreating Period Style and Decorative Features in Your Garden*. London: Dorling-Kindersley in Association with the National Trust, 1989.

Russell, William Howard. *My Diary North and South*. New York: Harper Bros., 1863.

Schinz, Mariana. *Visions of Paradise*. New York: Stewart, Tabori and Chang, 1935.

Seebom, Caroline and Christopher Simon Sykes. *Private Landscapes: Creating Form, Vistas, and Mystery in the Garden*. New York: Clarkson Potter, 1989.

Stahls, Paul. *Plantation Homes of the Teche Country*. Gretna, Louisiana: Pelican Publishing Company, 1979.

Stewart, Mary B. *Gardening in New Orleans*. New Orleans: Robert L. Crager and Company, 1952.

Stewart, Mary B. *The Southern Gardener*. New Orleans: Robert L. Crager and Company.

Taylor, Jasmine, ed. *Conservatories and Garden Rooms*. London: Macdonald, 1985.

Thacker, Christopher. *The History of Gardens*. Berkley: University of California Press, 1979.

Trussler, John. *Elements of Modern Gardening: Or, the Art of Laying Out of Pleasure Grounds, Ornamenting Farms, and Embellishing Views Round About Our Houses*. 1784.

Turnbull, Martha. *Diaries, 1836–1895*. Unpublished diary. On loan from the Feliciana Corporation, Houston, to the Hill Memorial Library, Louisiana State University, Baton Rouge.

Verey, Rosemary. *Classic Garden Design*. London: Viking, 1984.

Welch, William C. *Antique Roses for the South*. Dallas: Taylor Publishing Company, 1990.

Welch, William C. *Perennial Garden Color*. Dallas: Taylor Publishing Company, 1989.

Wood, Dennis. *Terrace and Courtyard Gardens*. Newton Abbot, England: David & Charles, 1970.

A List of Gardens

THE FOLLOWING LIST OF GARDENS IS PROVIDED TO GIVE ADDITIONAL INFORMATION ON SOME OF THE GARDENS AND GROUNDS WHICH ARE FEATURED IN THIS BOOK. WHILE MANY ARE OPEN TO THE PUBLIC YEAR-ROUND, OTHERS ARE OPENED ONLY SEASONALLY AND ON SPECIAL OCCASIONS, SUCH AS DURING SPRING AND FALL PILGRIMAGES. EACH SHOULD BE CONTACTED DIRECTLY TO OBTAIN INFORMATION ON SCHEDULES WHEN THE GARDENS ARE OPEN TO THE PUBLIC.

AFTON VILLA • 1790–1849

Located on U.S. Highway 61 four miles north of St. Francisville, Louisiana, the gardens comprise approximately thirty acres of meticulously maintained grounds. The original plantation was settled by the Barrow family from North Carolina. The gardens, which are built on seven terraces, have undergone many changes since 1790. Extensive reconstruction, designed by the late Mr. and Mrs. Theodore E. Landry, landscape architects, took place in the mid- to late 1950's.

THE BURN • 1835

Among the oldest Greek Revival houses in Natchez, The Burn is located on North Union Street. This four-acre site includes beautifully terraced gardens with many fine garden embellishments in the form of water, statuary, and old garden plants. Much of the work here was done by Mr. and Mrs. S.B. Laub, who purchased the property in 1935.

CHEROKEE • 1794–1810

Sitting atop a steep hill with an imposing view, Cherokee is located in the center of Natchez and includes a picturesque rear garden.

THE COTTAGE • 1795–1859

Located on U.S. Highway 61, nine miles north of St. Francisville, the Cottage includes a series of original buildings in the Spanish tradition. An original greenhouse is a special garden feature on this historic site.

DUNLEITH • 1856

Located in the heart of Natchez, this is among the most photographed houses in all America. Standing stately on a terrace of forty acres, the mansion has twenty-six Tuscan columns surrounding the house. The parklike grounds include an original poultry house topped with a *pigeonnier* and other original dependency buildings. A new formal garden was added in 1981.

ELMS COURT • 1810

Located on John R. Junkin Drive in Natchez, this house of Georgian architecture is sited on 150 acres of land and is approached by a long drive lined by both native and introduced plants. Many of the moss-covered plants—crape myrtles, oaks, and magnolias—have been a feature of this naturalistic garden since the house was built.

GREEN LEAVES • 1838

Located on North Rankin in Natchez, this historic house and grounds are noted for their mammoth, legendary live oaks.

HOUMAS HOUSE • 1840

Once among the largest sugar plantations in the region, this magnificent mansion is located on River Road (Louisiana Highway 30) near Burnside. The house and fine examples of dependency buildings are sited among stately live oaks. In recent years, the gardens have undergone extensive renewal under the direction of New Orleans landscape architect James Fondren.

LINDEN • 1785

Located on Melrose Avenue in Natchez, Linden is on the site of an original Spanish land grant. The beautiful spacious grounds contain magnificent trees as well as many old, nineteenth-century plants.

LIVE OAK • 1808

Reported to be one of the oldest houses in Louisiana, this West Feliciana Parish Live Oak (there are others in Louisiana) is located near the community of Weyanoke on Louisiana Highway 66. A grand avenue of over two-century-old live oaks and the beautiful grounds are special features of this site. Landscape architect Suzanne Turner has designed the most recent additions to the gardens.

LONGUE VUE HOUSE AND GARDENS • 1935

A New Orleans, eight-acre estate garden, located at 7 Bamboo Road, was built by the late Edith and Edgar Stern. The original garden, begun in 1935, was designed by Ellen Biddle Shipman, noted eastern U.S. landscape architect, with major revisions designed by eminent architect William Platt in 1965.

LOUISIANA STATE CAPITOL GROUND

Likely the most frequently visited gardens in the region are those occupying the grounds of the Louisiana State Capitol in Baton Rouge. The formal, highly patterned gardens were planted in 1932 by the firm of E.A. McIlhenney Jungle Gardens, Inc. of Avery Island, Louisiana. The original garden consisted of over 12,000 plants of 386 varieties at a cost of $108,000.

MAGNOLIA MOUND • 1791

Located on Nicholson Drive in the heart of Baton Rouge, this house and grounds built by the Duplantier family was once the hub of a huge plantation operation. Today it is a museum and center for the study of early plantation life. Splendid live oaks, a working kitchen garden, and several dependency buildings are the main features of the site. Landscape architect Jon Emerson has

received national recognition for the design of the kitchen garden and other recent work on the site.

MISTLETOE • 1807

This quaint plantation home nine miles north of Natchez in the Pine Ridge community includes beautiful grounds and a courtyard with many early garden plants.

MONMOUTH • 1818

Located on John A. Quitman Parkway in Natchez, the mansion sits atop a hill on a twenty-six-acre parklike site. The detailed gardens at the rear of the house are among the finest of all the Natchez homes. The gardens include a large collection of beautiful seasonal flowering plants, several fine garden structures, and outstanding construction details.

NOTTOWAY • 1857

The largest plantation home in the region, Nottoway is located on the River Road (Louisiana Highway 405) near White Castle, Louisiana. The imposing sixty-four-room, 53,000-square-foot mansion sits in a grove of stately live oaks. Extensive renovation began in 1980 with garden renewal currently underway.

OAK ALLEY • 1832–1836

Noted for its one-fourth mile alley of twenty-eight mammoth live oaks over 250 years old, Oak Alley is located adjacent to the Mississippi River on Louisiana Highway 18 near Vacherie, Louisiana. The beautiful informal, English countrysidelike grounds include many garden embellishments from the late nineteenth century.

OAKLEY HOUSE AND GROUNDS • 1808

Located on Louisiana Highway 965, near St. Francisville, this historic site is where the renowned artist and naturalist John James Audubon painted some of his most famous bird works. Now a part of the Louisiana State Parks system, it is a major commemorative area where the story of the mid-nineteenth-century plantation life is interpreted. The collection includes some of the earliest gardening tools used by the settlers. An original hothouse, formal garden, and dependency buildings are special features of the site.

PARLANGE • 1750

Located on Louisiana Highway 1 on False River near New Roads, Louisiana, this house, built by some of the earliest Louisiana settlers, has remained in the same family for seven generations. The informal, romantic garden was designed by Steele Burden and planted by the present owners, Mr. and Mrs. Walter Parlange. Some of the largest live oaks in the region are located on this plantation.

ROSALIE • 1820

No house in America is more beautifully sited than Rosalie, the Georgian mansion sitting atop the bluff overlooking the mighty Mississippi River in Natchez. The newly renovated gardens, which are filled with many of the old plants of the South, are among the most attractive of any of the historic Natchez houses.

ROSEDOWN • 1836

Located at the intersection of U.S. Highway 61 and Louisiana Highway 10 in St. Francisville, Louisiana, Rosedown is the best preserved of the early gardens. The original garden was planned in the French style of the seventeenth century by Daniel and Martha Turnbull. The late Ralph Gunn, Houston landscape architect, was hired in 1956 by the late Catherine Fondren Underwood of Houston to restore the gardens.

RURAL LIFE MUSEUM AND GARDENS

The 450-acre tract of land located at the intersection of U.S. Highways I-10 and I-12 in the heart of Baton Rouge, the Burden Research Plantation includes a large informal garden designed and planted by Steel Burden, who began his work here in 1930. The museum complex includes over twenty original buildings of the early twentieth-century plantation era. Each is completely furnished with original artifacts of everyday rural life.

SAN FRANCISCO • 1856

Noted for its "Steamboat Gothic" architecture, this magnificent house is located on Louisiana Highway 44 on the Mississippi River near Reserve, Louisiana. The old cistern is the major feature of the recently renovated grounds.

STANTON HALL • 1857

Located at 401 High Street in Natchez, the stately antebellum mansion and well-maintained grounds comprise an entire city block in the heart of this historic river city. The white stuccoed mansion is surrounded by huge live oaks, and the site includes a new rose garden.

TEZCUCO • 1855

This antebellum Greek Revival house and gardens are located on the Mississippi River on Louisiana Highway 44 near Darrow, Louisiana. The informal grounds, which include many old plantation buildings and garden structures, have an avenue of century-old live oaks in addition to plantings of magnolias, azaleas, and camellias giving a cathedral effect to the grounds.